"*Simply Tuesday* has done my soul a world of good. It's a beautiful invitation to slow down, embrace our smallness and our ordinary moments, and to enjoy the company of our Creator in each one. It's helped me to know how to live out the song I sang as a child, 'This is the day that the Lord has made! I will rejoice and be glad in it.' This book is like a deep breath for my soul."

—**Ellie Holcomb**, Dove Award–winning singer/songwriter

"We live in a time where we are led to believe that everything bigger is better and something in my soul has been telling me for a while now that isn't necessarily the case. And that's why I am so thankful for Emily Freeman's new book, *Simply Tuesday*. Emily has a way of putting an idea on the page in a way that is heartfelt and authentic and paints a picture that you've seen in your head but been unable to articulate. *Simply Tuesday* is a call to appreciate the small, simple things in life, and as I read it I found myself breathing a deep sigh of relief and nodding my head yes and basically underlining every other sentence. Do yourself a favor and read this call to simplicity by Emily. You won't regret a minute of it!"

—**Melanie Shankle**, *New York Times* bestselling author of *Nobody's Cuter Than You*

"In a world where bigger, better, faster, and louder are celebrated and valued, it may seem silly to go on a search for smallness. *Simply Tuesday* proves why such a journey is not only important, but is vital to a fulfilling existence. Within the pages of this beautifully crafted book, Emily Freeman reveals how the kingdom of God can be found in the ordinary days, quiet moments, openhanded surrenderings, and honest confessions. Whether you are looking for meaningful standards of success, relief from worldly comparison and pressure, or direction for your lost soul, *Simply Tuesday* promises a journey with great rewards."

—**Rachel Macy Stafford**, *New York Times* bestselling author of *Hands Free Mama*

"It doesn't hold the thrill of a new beginning or the anticipation of almost-finished. It's simply Tuesday. An ordinary day filled with beautiful, breathtaking moments I missed, until Emily Freeman taught me how to see. Through small-moment living, my hurried heart is learning how to slow down and savor. How to search less and find more. How to leave margin in my schedule and sacred space in my days to let my soul breathe. If you are tired of wanting more while secretly longing for less, this book is for you!"

—**Renee Swope**, bestselling author of *A Confident Heart*;
Proverbs 31 Ministries' Radio cohost of
Everyday Life with Lysa & Renee

"For years, my vision for Larry has been that he live more **settled,** grounded in his identity in Christ and in his calling from Christ." (Rachael)

"And my vision for Rachael, an ongoing prayer, is that she **rest,** aware that nothing she does deepens that beauty of her already Christ-revealing soul. We sense that heeding Emily's counsel to live on Tuesday, slowing down enough to experience life's small moments, will move us toward those visions. *Simply Tuesday* could move you toward the settled rest that Jesus provides." (Larry)

—**Dr. Larry Crabb**, author of *Fully Alive*;
director of NewWay Ministries

—**Rachael Crabb**, coauthor of *Listen In: Building Faith and Friendship through Conversations That Matter*

"Emily Freeman is a compassionate friend on the journey. Her gentle words and charming spirit shine a warm and glittery light on all that is beautiful in our ordinary days and our everyday ways. What if there is blessing in the way of small beginnings? What if God takes great delight in the simple acts of bench-sitting and gate-opening and being kind to our next-door neighbor? What if the kingdom of God is built on tiny, little gestures on simple days like Tuesday? Emily invites us to consider the grace in God's counterculture invitation to embrace small things; things like the one-inch living of a simple Tuesday. This book is a delight and a gift."

—**Deidra Riggs**, author of *Every Little Thing*;
blogger at *Jumping Tandem*

"Emily Freeman is a writer after my own heart. She's not afraid to be quiet, to move at a leisurely pace, and to think probably a little too hard about things. She believes that meaning and delight and revelation are found in the small moments. Her writing will slow you down, help your soul exhale, and show you that Tuesday, and every ordinary day, is full of magic."

—**Adam S. McHugh**, author of *The Listening Life: Embracing Attentiveness in a World of Distraction*

"Many of us are living at an unhealthy pace. We run from one task to another to another. We end up skimming the surface of life. This book challenges us to be present in the moments that we find ourselves in, and to live at depth with others."

—**Dave Runyon**, coauthor of *The Art of Neighboring*

"Emily Freeman writes like a trusted friend and speaks countercultural good news to all of us. In a society where more is more, her desire to celebrate her 'smallness' is refreshing and inspires us to pay attention to what God is doing in the ordinary everyday of our lives. I deeply resonated with these themes."

—**Jill Phillips**, Dove Award–winning singer/songwriter

Simply
TUESDAY

Books by Emily P. Freeman

Grace for the Good Girl
Graceful (for young women)
A Million Little Ways
Simply Tuesday

Simply TUESDAY

Small-Moment Living
in a Fast-Moving World

eMILY P. FREeMAN

Revell

a division of Baker Publishing Group
Grand Rapids, Michigan

© 2015 by Emily P. Freeman

Published by Revell
a division of Baker Publishing Group
P.O. Box 6287, Grand Rapids, MI 49516-6287
www.revellbooks.com

Printed in the United States of America

Library of Congress Cataloging-in-Publication Data
Freeman, Emily P., 1977–
    Simply Tuesday : small-moment living in a fast-moving world / Emily P.
    Freeman.
        pages cm
    Includes bibliographical references.
    ISBN 978-0-8007-2245-6 (pbk.)
    1. Christian life. I. Title.
    BV4501.3.F7393 2015
    248.4—dc23   2015014643

Published in association with the literary agency of Fedd & Company, Inc., PO Box 341973, Austin TX 78734.

15   16   17   18   19   20   21   7   6   5   4   3   2   1

green
press
INITIATIVE

To my Tuesday people in Greensboro
with love and gratitude,
for saving a seat on the bench

CONTENTS

INTRODUCTION

One Inch above the Ground

When Jesus said to seek first the kingdom of God, where did he intend for us to look? And how will we know when we've found it?

Certainly I won't find it here, in my home office with the unswept rug, my unwashed hair, and a to-do list that outnumbers the stars. And yet, that seems to be exactly where Jesus pointed when the Pharisees asked him when the kingdom of God would come.

Specifically, he answered them this way: "The coming of the kingdom of God is not something that can be observed, nor will people say, 'Here it is,' or 'There it is,' because the kingdom of God is in your midst" (Luke 17:20–21 NIV).

Someone once pointed out to me how, even though we always think of heaven as up—beyond the clouds, above the weather, and over the rainbow—it may not actually be *far* up.

"What if," this person wondered, "heaven is simply one inch above the ground?"

It's still up, but it's not so far away. Instead the kingdom of God exists right here in the moments where we live.

On some level, we already know this. Maybe you, like me, can recount moments in your life where it seemed you stepped through the invisible curtain dividing heaven and earth, where you nodded your head with misty eyes and thoughtful gaze, feeling the gauzy weight of eternity settle over the moment—at the wedding, the graduation, the birth of a baby, or even after a meaningful night with friends.

You already know life is sacred. You know the moments count. You know that most of the tasks on your to-do lists aren't all that important in the scheme of things.

And yet.

The constant buzzing inside your soul won't seem to quit.

That tight spot between your shoulders won't smooth out.

You know you need to slow and savor, but you're waiting until you finish this project or have that conversation or meet those people or achieve that success or finalize those decisions or get things organized.

By now I know the allure of hustle, how it feels both like winning and losing at the same time. As I watch the world move fast around me, I'm unsettled with all the ways I've adopted her pace. I talk fast, I walk fast, and I can finish tasks quickly when I need to. I've trained myself to ship and produce. At what cost? I'm not yet sure.

I'm thirty-seven years old, married to John for fourteen years, a mother of three, twin girls, Ava and Stella, who are eleven and a son, Luke, who is eight. I work from home writing books while my kids go to public school. I realize how simple that sounds, how dreamy actually. But make no mistake. While I may have a lot yet left to learn, one thing I know for sure is the language of the game, the pull to comparison and competition, the feeling that the work I do is never quite enough. I know the pain of inefficiency, the addiction of ambition, the longing to build something important, and the disappointment that comes when the outcome looks different than I thought.

And the outcome nearly always looks different than I thought.

I really do believe that the presence of Christ makes a difference in my everyday life. But sometimes I forget. And when I forget, I try hard to keep up. Even while I am mildly successful at it at times, I'm also aware of a natural slowness deep within me that I'm either thankful for or fight against, depending on the day. If there's a movement, a buzz, or a current event happening around me, it often takes me so long to process my opinions and perspectives that by the time I've formed some, the movement has moved on, the buzz has died down, and the event is no longer current.

If there were a magazine dedicated to year-old events, I would be the proud, slow-moving editor-in-chief. I have to read lines in books several times before I can figure out why they made me cry. Conversations have to be sifted through over a period of days, even a week, before I'm certain if I was fully myself in them or not. The lessons I've learned in my life haven't been showy, glitzy, headline-worthy, or viral material. Instead, they've happened one small step at a time—a shift here, a conversation there, the same prayers over and over again.

Sometimes I worry I miss out on opportunities because of this. When I'm alone and haven't had enough sleep and have spent too much time on the internet, I wish I were different—more edge, less curve.

While I can get worked up and start pointing my fingers at all the ways the world values the great, the noisy, and the next big thing, I'm hearing a whispered invitation pointing into the center of my own soul—where have I adopted these systems for myself?

In my exhaustion with this fast-moving world—the one that moves around me and the one that pounds within me—I turn to Jesus. "Hustle, produce, and ship" is not what I see in him.

My tendency is to turn my back on the world, to turn away, and to become critical. As I confess my own judgment of big-time living, I see that though the way of Jesus is different from the way of the world, his way is actually *all about the world.*

Jesus does not turn away from the world, but turns to face it. Jesus came down. He turns toward. He makes his face to shine upon. He shows compassion. He sits with. His with-ness is so important that every time we say his name, we declare it—Immanuel, God with us.

The way I have begun to practice confronting these systems within me is to do one of the most counterintuitive things I can think of: to remember my own smallness. And to not only tolerate it but to begin to look for it. In my search for smallness, I'm finding the kingdom of God one inch above the ground.

It doesn't look like I thought it would or think it should, but there it is, hiding under the piles of everyday life. God is where he always said he would be—in the whisper, in the shadows, in the seed.

I'm paying attention to the small ways that Jesus—and his kingdom—shows up in the daily ordinary, in the actual places where I live. When I think of where to find "the kingdom of God in our midst," Tuesday comes to mind. This is the day of the week housing the regular, the ordinary, the plain, and the small.

Most of life happens, not in brightness or in darkness, but in the medium light of a regular day. And all those daily things—the email inbox, the cluttered surfaces, the bag of old clothes, the deadlines, and the appointments—aren't to be set aside by those who hope to live a faithful life. Rather, embracing all of these is part of what *makes* a faithful life.

These regular tasks are the unlikely portals into the kingdom of God, and the goal isn't to set them aside but to recognize Christ with us in the midst of them.

The deepest need of my soul isn't a personal organizer or an empty inbox. The deepest need of my soul is Christ. But the problem is, I often forget where to find him.

What if God's intention for the world and me begins here, on my regular Tuesdays?

What if we decided to take back Tuesday from the wasteland of to-do lists and give it a prominent place in our walk of faith?

What if, instead of thinking we have to choose between our ordinary life and an extraordinary life, we began to realize they're the same thing?

What if we stopped asking God for big ways to serve him and started walking with our friend Jesus into the next simple moment in front of us?

I have a vision of a generation of believers who understand that the goal of life is Jesus and all the ways he wants to offer himself both to us and through us to the world.

I have a vision of people who make the invisible kingdom visible, sinking low to the ground, picking up our crosses and shoes off the floor, eating the bread of life and serving it up with peanut butter and jelly.

I have a vision of people who embrace the significance of our small words, knowing that whether they're spoken into microphones or near microwaves, they are all sacred when said in the power of the Spirit.

Let's take back quiet conversation with friends, whispered prayer over sick babies, belly laughter around the dinner table.

Let's take back the honor of small donations, small care packages, and small movements toward fellow image-bearers, because love isn't measured in inches, grand gestures, or dollar amounts.

Let's dare to take back that time when someone's words made us feel stupid, but instead of wallowing in the shame of it, we'll push through to the other side because directly after that painful conversation you saw a glimpse of strength and courage within you that wasn't there before and you have her to thank for it.

Let's take back the long days and the short years and all the months that come between them, because this is where our real life happens. And we won't be so naive as to try to make the hard times beautiful, but we will have faith that the hard days are making us, remaking us, and forming us into the likeness of Christ.

Let's take back moments that are lovely even if they are imperfect, words that are powerful even if only one person hears them, company that is meaningful even when we don't say any words at all.

Let's take back fame, the kind that comes from being born in a stable and teaching on a seashore and feeding up lunch to thousands from just a few loaves and fish; the kind of fame that comes from loving and saving the whole wide beautiful world.

Let's take it all back, these moments we've given away, thrown out with the leftovers and the papers we didn't think we needed. We left them behind in our pursuit of bigger and better and we've forgotten what's best.

We've been tricked into believing that higher up and further on equals impact and importance. And even those of us who don't *really* believe that still wince through the not-growing pains, when outcomes don't come out the way we hoped.

Maybe your small job with its small income leaves you feeling like you have a small influence.

Maybe you are discouraged because your small perspective and small vision has led you to believe you have a small faith.

Maybe your small house with your small people has somehow convinced you that you are too small to matter.

Maybe your small ministry in your small town gathers only a small group of people.

If hustle has hijacked your soul, listen up and listen well. *You're in good company here.*

In my own life I've found it to be true that when I hold on to the wrong things, the wrong things hold on to me.

If the light of a Tuesday morning candle isn't bright enough to light the room, a spotlight won't be either.

If the home where we live on Tuesday doesn't satisfy, we'll find ourselves always searching but never quite finding.

If the work we do on Tuesday doesn't feel important, we'll find ourselves slaves to comparison, forgetting compassion.

If the people we live our lives with now aren't sacred companions for us, we'll find ourselves competing with everyone and connecting with no one.

If our souls long for more and bigger and refuse the Tuesday way, how will we ever fully share in the life of Christ who became less and arrived small?

If we parcel out our time and hold our plans in a vice-grip of what shall, will, and must be for our future, we may dismiss the small beginnings being born right here, on Tuesday afternoon. We'll be pushed around by fear rather than be led by love.

Attention, success, and comparison hold my soul hostage and refuse to negotiate until they get what they want.

Spoiler alert: They want everything. And they are never satisfied. They will never let you go.

We need a rescuer to come and save us from the bondage of the lie that whispers we have to build and grow and be known by all.

The good news is we have one. The better news is he's already come. And the best news is he keeps showing up on our everyday Tuesdays, one inch above the ground.

As it turns out, Jesus doesn't come riding in on a white horse to save me from my humiliation, my daily work, my endless list. Instead, he whispers a quiet invitation to keep company with him the way he came to earth to keep company with us. It won't always feel like a rescue. It might feel like surrender. But on the other side of that space I find Jesus. I find his peace. I find his companionship.

Let's be people of the kingdom, the kind who have faith the size of mustard seeds and influence like the salt on our dinner plate. Jesus came to earth to extend a personal invitation for us to enter into his kingdom rather than try to build our own. Because his kingdom is with us and, more importantly, *within us*, the best place to find it is right where we are, on our regular Tuesdays. And the best people to reveal his kingdom to us are the Tuesday people in our midst.

I'm exploring what it looks like to release my obsession with building a life and embrace the life Christ is building in me, one small Tuesday at a time. I hope you'll come along.

Part I

Discovering Our TUESDAY Home

Less searching. More finding.

To be rooted is perhaps the most important and least recognized need of the human soul. It is one of the hardest to define. A human being has roots by virtue of his real, active and natural participation in the life of a community which preserves in living shape certain particular treasures of the past and certain particular expectations for the future.

—Simone Weil, *The Need for Roots*

In this section, you are invited to:

- see your smallness as a gift and not a liability
- discover home right where you are
- release the obsession with building a life
- trust in the life Christ is building in you

CITIES & BENCHES

An Accidental Sighting
of the Kingdom of God

Night: we cannot stop it, or hasten it; it just comes, and
it teaches us every twenty-four hours that we are not in
complete control.

—Father Iain Matthew, *The Impact of God*

In January 1994, an earthquake lasting up to twenty seconds
hit the San Fernando Valley region of Los Angeles, California, causing nearly twenty billion dollars in damages and
the deaths of nearly sixty people. Much of the city's power
was lost because of the quake; radio and television stations
were knocked off the air. That night, the Griffith Observatory
in Los Angeles began to receive odd phone calls from panicked
citizens reporting a "strange sky." They speculated that perhaps
the silver cloud above them somehow caused the earthquake.

After some confusion, the director of the observatory realized what was going on. With the city lights made powerless by the earthquake, for the first time maybe ever, the people living in Los Angeles looked up and saw a dark sky.

The scary, smoky, silver cloud they reported was the Milky Way. Today, two-thirds of the United States population and one-fifth of the world can't even see it.

> A clear view of the solar system—and that awesome, unmooring, sublime, occasionally terrifying feeling that comes over us when we bear witness to the vastness of the universe and recognize our infinitesimal place in it—had been a routine nocturnal experience for the bulk of human history. Now it's become rarefied and, for some, unimaginable.[1]

When I first read this article in *Men's Journal* last December, I laughed out loud. Those crazy people! Calling the observatory about the spooky cloud in the sky! Haven't they ever seen the Milky Way?

Wait a minute. I've never seen the Milky Way. It was a sobering realization. While I laughed at the citizens of Los Angeles only moments before, now I wondered if I too would have called the observatory with questions about the strange cloud in the sky. I considered the connection between the fast pace of my soul and my inability to see the stars at night. If I had a more regular reminder of my size on earth, would I live differently as a result?

My City Lights

I am a lover of the light. If I told you how many lamps are on in my house right now, well, let's just say Al Gore might show up at my door and shake a finger in my face. Maybe I feel safer that way, with all the lights on.

I walk outside, the porch light spilling onto the yard. I am in control of my surroundings. After all, I can see my porch, the driveway, and part of our street. In a way I haven't fully appreciated or understood, the manufactured artificial light numbs the mystery of the dark, giving me a false sense of myself in relation to the world.

The way I move through my world on a daily basis is mostly efficient. And when it isn't, I have a little niggling in the back of my mind that I needlessly wasted time today. I know how to hustle, produce, and ship. But lately, I've had to honestly confront a real possibility: what if "hustle, produce, and ship" are my artificial lights?

I look up and see six stars, now seven. I am unaware. If I could turn the lights out, all the world's lights, how many stars would I see? One or two thousand? Five thousand on a moonless night? Would seeing them be enough to remind me I am small? Would I be relieved or would I close my eyes? Would I cry?

Several years ago I was struggling through a time of not understanding some things going on in my life, of being painfully misunderstood by some friends, and of beginning to feel the pressure of writing books, meeting deadlines, and hearing opinions on my work from strangers and friends alike.

I recognized within myself a deep desire to explain and defend my ideas, to be seen and heard for who I was, to grow my influence without selling my soul, and also to be able to somehow see a bigger picture of what it all meant. I was feeling the pain of smallness and I didn't like it. The lights were dim in my personal city and I wanted them to shine more brightly so I could find the answers I thought I needed.

It was in the midst of this struggle that a trusted mentor encouraged me with these strange words: "Celebrate your small-ness."[2] I wanted to see the big picture of my life and instead he told me to be small—not only to be small, but also to *celebrate it.*

If you're anything like me, then the word *small* may not bring to mind kind or encouraging images. We tend to associate feeling small with negative experiences. In fact, I recently did a highly scientific study on this word and the situations that cause people to feel so. I asked on Facebook: *What kinds of things, situations, people, or circumstances cause you to feel small?* Here are some of the most common answers I received:

Being new at something and having to perform it in front of others.

Being misunderstood.

Being wrong.

Being corrected.

Being ignored.

Being embarrassed.

Being single when it seems everyone else isn't.

Chaos.

Crowds.

Criticism.

Church people.

Women who look like they have it all together.

When work is unrecognized and passions are tossed aside by others.

When I'm first starting out.

When others know something I don't.

Sarcastic people.

When I think of feeling small, I mainly consider the kind that comes as a result of humiliation. These are the kinds of things we say when we feel rejected. When someone says something insulting or disrespectful, we say they belittle us, making us feel "about this big." (Hold up thumb and forefinger measuring an inch.) If people are stubborn or prejudiced, we call them small-minded. If your influence, vision, or dreams are small, you may be accused of being scared or lacking faith.

And then there are the more surface ways we use the word. We may feel discouraged if our house, our jeans, our portions, or our bank accounts are too small. *Small* becomes attached to *too*, and these two words together shape unwanted images within us: too small to satisfy, too small to have an impact, too small to be important, too small to make a difference, too small to see.

Small seems like the opposite of spacious, the opposite of enough, the opposite of free. All of these smalls lead to embarrassment, uncertainty, anxiety, or discontent. When this mentor of mine suggested I celebrate my smallness, I was thinking of it only in these kinds of terms—feeling lost, less-than, embarrassed, and alone. That doesn't sound like much of a celebration.

But these aren't our only experiences of smallness. In fact, in certain situations we experience a natural celebration of smallness.

When I asked the question on Facebook—*What kinds of things, situations, people, or circumstances cause you to feel small?*—several people asked the same clarifying question: *Do you mean the good kind of small or the bad kind of small?*

I am so glad they asked, because when I imagine what it means to feel small, other kinds of images come to mind as well. Here are some other answers I received that afternoon:

Creating art.

Standing near the ocean.

Looking at the stars.

When I'm trusted to care for children.

Walking through the woods.

When everything is covered in snow.

In his book *The Contemplative Pastor*, Eugene Peterson offers another perspective of small. "The metaphors Jesus used for the life of ministry are frequently images of the single, the small, and the quiet, which have effects far in excess of their appearance: salt, leaven, seed. Our culture publicizes the opposite emphasis: the big, the multitudinous, the noisy."[3]

Jesus pointed out that faith, not only as small as a seed but one of the smallest seeds of all—the mustard seed—was enough to move a mountain.

Creation invites a vastly different image to this word *small*. Driving toward the mountains, standing on the beach, sitting beneath the sky on a moonless night—I feel small, but I like it this way. It's comforting, like I'm not in control and I wouldn't want to be.

In these places, I'm small enough to breathe in deeply, small enough to see what's happening, and small enough to let go, to be loved, to remember the with-ness of Christ. This kind of small carries wonder, gratitude, and peace. This kind of small leads to worship.

Jesus was born in Bethlehem, small among Judah. He came as a baby, small among men. He began to build his kingdom in the womb of young Mary. Jesus himself arrived small on earth, but he was not insufficient or lacking in significance. Simply, he did not hold on to his own glory.

In her book *Shirt of Flame*, Heather King writes this: "I was reminded of contemplative theologian Richard Rohr's theory that the opposite of holding on isn't, as we tend to think, letting go—but rather participating in something greater than ourselves."[4]

Small is an invitation to participate in something greater than ourselves. Isn't this what Jesus did with his Father while on earth? Gave up his own glory so he could participate with the Father? In his smallness, Jesus wasn't attempting to build a city. He had his sights set much higher. Jesus was here to establish a kingdom and his foundation was the whole world. But even Jesus didn't seem to make it his business to grow it.

He constantly turned to his Father in everything, refusing to hold his own glory, walking as the most dependent man who ever lived. And now the Spirit of the most dependent man who ever lived has made his home in us.

Instead of forgetting or running from my own smallness, what if I chose instead to look it in the face, to settle down into the place where I am, to notice what is happening around me on my ordinary days? What if these small moments are the very portal into experiencing the kingdom of God? I believe they are—and if we miss them, we miss everything. We run right by the kingdom's doors, and no matter where we go, we have missed the door that leads us home.

The City Builders

In the Bible, Cain is a good example of someone who refused to consider his small place on earth and, in turn, missed the kingdom of God.

As grown sons of Adam and Eve, Cain works the ground while his brother, Abel, tends the animals. They both bring a sacrifice to the Lord; Cain brings fruit from the ground and Abel brings the best of his flock. Abel's sacrifice is more pleasing to God than Cain's, so Cain, in his jealousy, kills his brother and then gets caught.

In Genesis 4:12, God says these words to Cain: "When you cultivate the ground, it will no longer yield its strength to you; you will be a vagrant and a wanderer on earth."

And then comes what is to me one of the most heartbreaking verses thus far in Scripture: "Then Cain went out from the presence of the LORD, and settled in the land of Nod, east of Eden" (Gen. 4:16).

In his book *The Meaning of the City*, Jacques Ellul emphasizes the now homelessness of Cain. "Cain no longer has a home, either human or geographical, because murder destroys the home. And he who no longer has a home is condemned to death. A fugitive and a wanderer, he is even worse off than someone already in the grave."[5]

Cain has made a turn from which there is no going back. Taking his cues from his own idea of what home, security, and power should look like, he sets out to find security on his own terms and of his own making, apart from God. He enters into the land of Nod, the land of wandering, to begin his life.

Cain and his wife do two things after leaving the presence of God. First, they have a son, and second, they build a city. Cain gives both their son and the city the same name: Enoch, meaning "initiation" or "dedication."

Ellul says this about the significance of Cain's decision to have a child and build a city: "The first builder of a city thinks of his action as a response to his situation, an effort to satisfy his deepest desires. He will satisfy his desire for eternity by producing children, and he will satisfy his desire for security by creating a place belonging to him, a city."[6]

As much as I would like to distance myself from the choices Cain made, in a way I understand how building a city seems like the next right thing to do. City building keeps our souls occupied, our hands moving, and our hearts distracted. Cities are exciting and filled with activity. City building helps us forget what our souls most long for.

Our souls weren't made to live without acceptance, without a home. But sin takes us to places we were never meant to go. And since living with rejection isn't an option, we must find acceptance at any price. When our souls lose home, we set out to build a new home.

We start with a strange mix of raw materials: talent, skill, and hustle. We'll use whatever we've got: strength, wisdom, beauty, and humor. We build this home up with lights and action, bustle and distraction, filled with satisfaction. For a while. But then, a fissure. A shift in the market. An earthquake. Unemployment. A heartbreak. A death. A grief that rolls right over you. And the lights of the city go out and we don't recognize ourselves anymore. Where are my bearings? And what are those lights in the sky? Now a new kind of crisis settles in, the panic kind. Because I cannot continue in my own life when I feel this small. It hurts too much.

To be like Cain is to turn from God and establish my own city. I've done this in various ways—in my home, in my work, with my family, in my soul, and with my time.

I want to allow the Spirit to uncover the ways I've laid out my own blueprints over these sacred parts of my life. I want to invite him to take my hammer and my nails and, instead, bring me to a place to sit.

The Bench Dwellers

Our house sits at the top of a cul-de-sac, nestled between one neighbor who has lived here over forty-five years and a retired couple who have been here only a few years longer than we have. On the other side of that couple are John's brother, Frank, his wife, Mercedes, and their two young girls. They moved here first, and a few years later when this house had sat empty for a while, they suggested we try to buy it. After some stuff and things and negotiating, we did.

Our kids and our nieces were still riding tricycles at the time, so we often sat outside in the grassy center of the cul-de-sac to watch. Other kids from down the street would often come to join in, and John, Frank, Mercedes and I pulled out lawn chairs from the garage or spread out blankets on the grass to watch the kids play.

One afternoon while John's mom was visiting, she mentioned how nice it would be to have a couple of benches in the center of the circle, more permanent seating so we wouldn't always have to drag our lawn chairs out every time the kids wanted to play. Not one to suggest ideas without taking responsibility, she showed up several days later with a bench in a box in the back of her car. Days later, a neighbor bought a matching one.

Now we have two benches facing each other in front of our houses, like our little community of seven homes finally has a living room.

As I was preparing dinner one afternoon, I glanced out my kitchen window and noticed three of our neighbors leave their homes at nearly the same time, making their way at various shuffling speeds to meet at the benches in the middle.

I'd seen them outside in the past, chatting over newly fetched mail or exchanging comments about the weather, but they had never stayed out for more than a few minutes as their aging bodies wouldn't cooperate with the demands of standing for so long. Now that we had benches, everything was different. Unable to resist the community, I went outside to check the mail and crossed the street to talk with them for a few moments. We spoke of children and grandchildren, aging siblings and friends, the weather. We enjoyed the breeze and waved at the occasional passing car. We lingered.

With dinner still cooking inside, I made my way back to the kitchen but kept my eye on them through my window. They stayed out for nearly an hour. I'd not seen them do that before. It wasn't that they didn't want to be together, but before it wasn't so easy. Now they had benches to sit on. And the benches made all the difference.

The benches didn't give them something to talk about. The benches weren't fancy, expensive, impressive, or flashy. They weren't a complicated solution to an unsolvable problem, and they didn't offer answers to difficult questions. The benches simply gave us neighbors a place to be, a place to rest, a place to come together on an ordinary day.

I've thought of this often in many areas of life when I try to make things too complicated. When I feel myself getting carried away, when I feel tempted to turn and build a city rather than accept my right-now home, I ask this simple question: *Where is the bench in this moment?*

In my work, when I see all the reasons why what they're doing over there is more important, impactful, and effective than what I'm doing over here, I'm tempted to make the plat-form wider and put brighter lights in the bulbs because I have to dazzle, you know. I am determined to make my work the best, the most excellent. When I want to climb the ladder, what if instead I tore the ladder apart and used the wood to build a bench?

In my relationships, when I see a need I think needs fixing, a conversation I don't know how to tackle, a grief I have no words for, I'm tempted to make things complicated and fast-moving—let's pull out the city plans, build the roadways and sidewalks straight to your heart. But people don't need fancy and flashy, they probably just want regular. They don't need a fixer, they need a journeyer. They just need to sit on a bench with someone else so they know they're not alone. I know this because it's what I need too.

In my own soul, when I feel the need rise up in me for recognition, appreciation, and validation; when I feel my soul grasp and grope for worth, significance, a city to call my own, I want to look for the bench instead. *How can I sit down on the inside?*

A city is big and bright, loud and fast, important. A bench is small, quiet, and still with only enough room for a few.

Let's look beyond our first impressions of the bench as a place only for the players who aren't skilled enough to start, the second-string, the substitutes, the leftovers, the lazy, the overwhelmed, and the overlooked.

Let's explore city building and bench dwelling and be willing to allow the lights to go out in the city and see what we find above, around, and within us.

In our society, city lights are proof of life, progress, and growth; a sign of privilege, productivity, and opportunity. But when we bring all this to the inner life, the city lights we burn in our souls can begin to overpower the hidden life in Christ.

What happens when we are required to walk through darkness? What happens when we can't see our way? What happens when we don't know answers to our soul's deepest questions or the questions of those around us? The temptation is to start to build a city right there, a plan to find the answers, to fix the problem, to light the darkness once more.

But Christ himself is the light and any light I try to manufacture outside of him will be a false light at best. He has called me to a life of burden bearing and by-faith walking. Co-suffering, co-death, co-burial.

These are not the city way. These are the way of the lowly, the criminal, and the marginalized. But the mystery of Christ in you is that there, on the bench, God ushers you into his kingdom.

> Or have you forgotten that when we were joined with Christ Jesus in baptism, we joined him in his death? For we died and were buried with Christ by baptism. And just as Christ was raised from the dead by the glorious power of the Father, now we also may live new lives. Since we have been united with him in his death, we will also be raised to life as he was. (Rom. 6:3–5 NLT)

So what is this new life? It is relief that comes from learning to lean back into small-moment living rather than trying to keep pace with a fast-moving world.

When confronted with heartbreak, fear, questions, longing, frustrations, and grief, this new life means instead of running to build our cities of protection, we can set out on a different road. This road that may include loneliness, obscurity, hiddenness, and silence. It may be narrow, lined with danger, and filled with darkness at times. But we have a light that will not go out and cannot be turned off. The light of Christ burns bright within us, and wherever we go we will not go alone. This is our promise, our protection, and the place where our voice comes from. When we turn our back on the city, we may find heartache—but we will also find something else.

We're headed down the new way of Christ, and all roads away from the city lead to the kingdom of God. The road to the kingdom is lined with invisible benches where the great work of love, service, listening, community, prayer, change, and transformation will occur.

Where to Look for the Kingdom of God

Everyone in my family was ready for church, already getting into our minivan. But I was running frantically through the house looking for my jacket. It wasn't in any of the normal places. I checked the top of the dresser, the floor beside my bed, the back of my office chair, and the dining room table. I nearly gave up and wore a different one, but on a crazy whim decided to check one last place—the closet.

There it was, hanging obediently in the one place it should have been, the one place it's supposed to actually be but rarely is because of my messy ways. And as I slipped on my jacket and ran out the door to join my family, I thought of how Jesus is often in the last place I want to look but the very place he always said he would be—in the whisper, in the children, in the small and secret places.

> The kingdom of God is like a man who scatters seed on the ground.
> The kingdom of God is like a mustard seed.
> The kingdom of God is like a net.

The kingdom of heaven is like yeast.

The kingdom of heaven is like a treasure hidden in a field.[7]

Permit the children to come to Me, and do not hinder them, for the kingdom of God belongs to such as these. (Luke 18:16)

Seeds, nets, yeast, a hidden treasure, a farmer, and a child—these are the clues to the kingdom. The road to the kingdom is available now; we walk on it every day even though we can't see it. God has set eternity in our hearts. We forget, but we know.

We don't have to fear this small way. We don't have to worry that embracing smallness will shrink our impact. Small was Jesus's whole life—how he came, how he lived, how he died, even to whom he revealed himself once he rose again.

Small is the position of my soul, the posture by which I approach others, God, and myself. When I'm small, I know I can't control opinions, manipulate outcomes, or force my agenda on others. When I'm small, I can move into the world confident as the person I most deeply am because I know I don't move into the world alone.

If this is true, then small is my new free.

But it won't always feel this way. Every day we are confronted with our own smallness. Those feelings of smallness come when we feel rejected, left out, afraid, overlooked. But they also show up when we stand at the edge of the ocean, on the top of a mountain or a building in the city, around the campfire with family.

We may make a distinction between the good kind of small and the bad kind of small, but the truth is there is no difference. In all our small ways, it is Christ who makes it possible for us to move through our lives, believing and trusting he is establishing his kingdom-sized purposes within and around us.

Small is our silent companion as we stand in a place of our own humiliation as well as in the midst of God's creation.

While humiliations may tempt us to build our own kingdoms, it's possible for us to let them prompt us to enter the kingdom of God, one inch above the ground. The same way Christ came small in Bethlehem, he continues to show up small within us, to establish his kingdom on earth.

It is my hope that when I'm finished writing this book (and you're finished reading it) we will hesitate to move so fast past those moments when we feel small and, instead, learn to sit with them. The same way the life of Christ was placed into the body of Mary, I want to discover how his life is being born within me. I want to practice seeing those small moments—both the ones that come from humiliation as well as those that are a result of creation—as secret entryways into the kingdom of God.

So where do we start our search for the kingdom of heaven? How do we discover our own benches and the benches we want to build for others? Let's begin on Tuesday, the smallest day of the week.

A Prayer for the Bench Dwellers

We confess our desire to light up our worlds with our own abilities, smarts, and accomplishments. May we have the courage to revisit our associations with the word *small*. May we be willing to change our minds about it, to decide to fold ourselves into it rather than run fast away. May we see our city plans for what they truly are—a steadfast dedication to ourselves. Instead, give us courage to sit on a bench and listen to the secrets small things have to teach us.

MOMENTS & TIME

Counting the Smallest Day of the Week

It is ingrained in us that we have to do exceptional things
for God—but we do not. We have to be exceptional in
the ordinary things of life, and holy on the ordinary
streets, among ordinary people—and this is not learned
in five minutes.

—Oswald Chambers, *My Utmost for His Highest*

The thing about being a citizen of an invisible kingdom
is that sometimes you can't find your way home. It isn't
that you don't believe you have a home; it's simply
invisible so you can't see it.

When we forget how to find our true home, it's good to
seek artists who help us remember, artists who know the same
familiar shapes and sounds, who can sing the sacred melodies

your soul recognizes, who can weave the stories that reflect the truth of God.

Sarah Masen is one of those artists for me.

I can still hear it in my mind, track seven on her self-titled album, the song called "Tuesday." I listened to it on repeat in college, three minutes and twenty-eight seconds looped around the room while I folded my clothes on a quiet Friday night, organizing my desk drawers and school binders. I was a party waiting to happen.

The song's words bounced off the white cinder-block walls—a song about a girl who was going through her day in a rush, too busy to pause and chat at the sky. I picture the girl the same way every time, tennis shoes and a pink T-shirt, pony-tail swinging, bag slung over her shoulder, fast-walking, head down. But that evening, she sees the sunset and can't help but notice it, to stand beneath it, and watch the greatness of it. Under the brilliant light of sky, a painting to close the day, she finally slows her fast movements to take a moment in the middle of an ordinary Tuesday to pause and choose to see. Her response is a profoundly poetic awareness of her own smallness.

Back in 2005 when I decided to start writing online, I chose an obscure blog platform, filled in all the required information, careful to use only my initials rather than my full name so as to avoid being stalked by all the killers lurking around the World Wide Web. I chose the colors I wanted to use and then came to an empty space where I was to type in a name, what I wanted to call the blog.

As I sat at the desk in the corner of the bedroom John and I had shared for four years as a married couple, laundry piled up behind me, one twin balanced on my left knee, the other crawling at my feet, this phrase from Sarah's song "Tuesday" came to mind immediately. I typed the words *chatting at the sky* into the blank and hit enter. Thus began my writing life.

Since then I've moved on from that first blogging platform, made many changes in both form and structure to my blog, but the heading under which I write has remained the same for ten years: *Chatting at the Sky*. It's a constant reminder to me to stop, to notice, to see.

I'm glad she called that song "Tuesday" because it's the long string of ordinary Tuesdays of our lives when we are most likely to forget to breathe, to be present, and to see evidence of the kingdom of God.

Tuesday is the eat-at-home day, the go-to-bed-early day, the routines-are-all-in-order day. Perhaps the most ordinary of all the days, Tuesday lacks the excitement of the weekend or the productivity of, say, Monday. Tuesday is business as usual, continuing on with the week. Tuesday is on the way, but not there yet. It's the just-getting-started day, the day we bring donuts to the office because it's going to be a long week. We don't schedule parties for Tuesday, but perhaps we'll send out the invitations.

Tuesday wears an acceptable shade of green, sensible shoes, and a pair of reading glasses. She may not get the job done but she's the one who continues doing it. Tuesday doesn't mess around, but neither does she bark orders. A deadline is coming, but not today. Today is simply Tuesday, so let's carry on and find out what she holds.

I recently heard an interview with Lorne Michaels, the creator of *Saturday Night Live* and the man partially responsible for launching the careers of Tina Fey, Will Ferrell, Bill Murray, and countless others. He has also produced several movies and other television shows. When it comes to being a producer, he says when he does his job right, he leaves no fingerprints.[1]

Tuesday is the week's producer. What happens here, if done right, if done well, leaves no fingerprints—dinner around the table, laundry folded in the baskets, the meeting with the boss over coffee, five hundred more words toward the deadline. The big stuff of life we save for the weekend. Tuesday holds the ordinary, the everyday, and the small.

The past few years have been for me a practice of embracing what I find on my Tuesdays. During a time when my kids were in preschool and the days all ran together, I started a weekly practice I called Tuesdays Unwrapped. I was nostalgic enough to know that one day I would probably miss those days but sleep-deprived enough to not be able to fully appreciate them.

So I decided to mark them, to celebrate on purpose the messy, the lovely, and the unexpected moments of life. The best way I could think of to do that was to write about them and then invite others to join me.

Every week, over one hundred women would write, unwrapping their Tuesday moments on their blogs, and every week, I remembered again how thankful I was to have a community to help me see the beauty hidden beneath the piles of to-do lists, diapers, and dirty clothes.[2]

Maybe it's an overused phrase, how we miss the living because we forget the moments. But the overused phrases get that way because they touch on something true, something needed, something we all want.

When it comes to paying attention to your real life, Tuesday seems to be the most logical place to look. Here is where you keep time, in this home with these people and this skin on. Here is the lamppost in your front yard that won't light because of the baseball that broke the glass last summer. Here is that closet you hate to organize, that drawer that still won't open, the bookshelf with all your favorite worlds waiting to be rediscovered. This is where we live for now, though maybe not forever. But here, on our ordinary Tuesdays, is where we make our homes and learn to be human.

If you ever come to our house, you will walk up the painted white steps of our front porch and be welcomed into the small foyer just inside the double doors. You will notice the doorway to our living room on your left, our dining room on your right, and the wooden stairs straight ahead.

Though the area is only large enough for a small group of people to stand in comfortably, our kids have found this open, furniture-free area to be the perfect spot for playing hand hockey. They actually call it just plain hockey, but they use their hands instead of sticks and a soft puck that may or may not have come in a happy meal once, so I don't want to mislead you by calling it real hockey. The opposite doorways to the living room and dining room serve as their goals. Two kids sit in front of their respective doorways to guard those goals with legs sprawled and arms up while the third sibling sits on the steps to act as the scorekeeper and referee.

I let them play inside because there isn't much that can break in the foyer with a soft puck, and also because they love it. But it gets loud in there, especially if there's a disagreement on whether or not the puck actually crossed the line into the "goal." And so the laughter and banter in the game is constantly punctured with loud, alternating protests of "That one counted!" or "No, it didn't! That one didn't count at all!"

Having something count is important. If the goal counts, your team might win. If it doesn't, you might be out. It may seem childish at first glance but I can relate. I want my time, money, efforts, and points to count too. Counting means something. Not counting feels like a waste.

The Kind of Days That Count

When I was growing up, the only two things I knew about the church calendar was that Christmas came on December 25 and Easter came in springtime. I didn't know anything about Lent or Epiphany and only had the faintest understanding of Advent.

Over the past several years, I've been learning more about the structure of the church year; about how our faith can grow as we follow the rhythms of time and that these rhythms have names and markings. Most recently I've been reading from a book by Kimberlee Conway Ireton called *The Circle of Seasons*. She explains that the church year, or liturgical year, is divided into two halves: "The first half, beginning in early December with the first Sunday of Advent and stretching till Pentecost in May or June, tells the story of the life of Christ. The second half, from Pentecost until Christ the King Sunday in late November, is the story of the church."[3]

The first half of the year includes Advent/Christmas/Epiphany and then Lent/Easter/Pentecost. "In each of these cycles, a season of preparation precedes a season of celebration and concludes with a special day of rejoicing. At the end of each cycle comes a season called Ordinary Time."[4]

After Epiphany comes the first cycle of Ordinary Time and the second follows Pentecost and goes all the way until Advent. If you add up the days of Ordinary Time, they make up more than half the church year.

You actually don't have to know much about the church calendar to realize how ordinary time can feel. We already know that most of life is ordinary without it being something official. But when I learned that these ordinary days of life had a name, when I learned that someone decided to mark not only Advent and Christmas, Lent and Easter but all the days that come between—that meant something to me, even if they are labeled as ordinary.

I smiled when I read these words by author Sarah Arthur: "If Advent, Lent, and Easter are the glitzy celebrities at the liturgical party, Ordinary Time is the plain auntie collecting dirty wine glasses afterward. We almost forget she's there."[5] The plain auntie cleaning up. I think we can all relate to her.

Wendy M. Wright offers another perspective on Ordinary Time in her book *The Time Between*, where she challenges our usual definition of the word *ordinary*. "It does not mean what you might think: boring, uneventful, undistinguished, everyday, ordinary. In fact, it means 'counted time.' The word *ordinary* comes from the word *ordinal*, to count."[6]

All these weeks of regular Tuesdays are not only named, *they count*.

On Living Well in Ordinary Time

I resonate with the quote at the beginning of this chapter, the one about how it's ingrained in us that we have to do exceptional things for God. Sometimes, though, I'm not sure it's God I want to do exceptional things for, but me. I want to do exceptional things for myself, for my name's sake, for my own reputation and exaltation. I want my Tuesdays to count for something more than ordinary, want my work to produce something that looks more like a city and less like a bench.

My favorite part of that quote, though, is that last line that says "and this is not learned in five minutes." I smile every time I read those words, because I feel like Oswald (may I call him Oswald?) is speaking like a grandfather, chin down, looking over the top of his glasses, telling me to be patient and to stop tapping my foot so much.

As hard as this is to admit, sometimes it's easier for me to have faith, to be patient, and to trust God in the midst of the big challenges of life because it is so obvious I'm not in control—the diagnosis, the job insecurity, the safety and well-being of my family. In these circumstances, it feels like my only choice for comfort, peace, or sleeping even a little at night is an unrelenting trust in God.

Instead, it's those everyday things that are covered with my fingerprints. During the repetitive minutiae of the daily is when my trusting soul seems to fall asleep in the brush, beneath the shade of the familiar trees and the warm landscape of everyday life. It isn't that I don't believe the small things are important; it's more that I forget to care about how important they are.

In her book *The Memoir Project*, author Marion Roach Smith said, "It's in the small moments that life is truly lived."[7] We've all heard some version of this. Maybe our minds immediately go to the wink across a crowded room, the snuggles before a bedtime story, the weeknight cookouts, and the daily dishes.

But our days aren't only filled with the beautiful ordinary.

If it's true what Marion Roach Smith says, that small moments are where life is truly lived, then we have to count *all* the small moments, not just the pleasant ones. The days also have small moments of rejection, humiliation, disappointment, regret, misunderstanding, heartache, and pain. These are our moments too. How we define "small moments" is crucial to seeing, embracing, and learning from our whole life, not just the pretty parts. These small moments can offer hints of a greater reality just like the lovely ones do. But in these, it can be harder to find.

A lot of us can probably relate to this inability to live well in the small moments. Perhaps one reason is because, as Eugene Peterson points out, "the world gives scant attention to what it means to *live*, to really live, to live eternal life in ordinary time."[8] I agree.

It's easy to fight for a cause when the stakes are high— freedom, rights, life or death. It's way harder to fight for moments, to fight to see meaning on a Tuesday afternoon around the homework table. Because at the end of it you don't have anything to show for it beyond a kid who has a finished math worksheet and let's be honest, who cares much about that?

Yet if the world gives it such little attention, maybe we need to crane our necks away from cities of the world and force our attention to the benches in our own front yards. I don't mean we have to create meaning and elevate each moment to the level of The Most Important Thing Ever. The truth is, the moments *may* be boring. In the scope of life, they may not have much impact on the course of things or the decisions we make. But learning to live well in ordinary time isn't a call to elevate moments; it's a call to draw close to Christ.

What gives moments meaning is not the moments themselves but the presence of Christ with us in the midst of them. To learn to live well in ordinary time is to keep company with Christ on our simple Tuesdays and remember how he delights in keeping company with us. It's to understand that the life of Christ dwells within me as I walk into the coffee shop, the courtroom, the office, the classroom, the shed. To live well in ordinary time is to believe within the deepest part of who I am that wherever I go, I don't go alone. That means when a word is spoken to me in love or criticism, in comfort or indifference, in truth or in falsehood, first it must go through my friend Jesus before it gets to me. Always standing between me and others is the presence of Christ—beside and within me. He packs the moments of Ordinary Time with the hope of Easter, the miracle of Advent, the light of Epiphany. But he does so in the middle of my Tuesday, one ordinary moment at a time.

Let's dig deep, not to create meaning where there isn't any, but to see Christ, our companion, where he actually is, not where we wish he was. Let's gently poke our sleepy souls, refusing to wait for a big event to wake us up. Let's stop running from ordinary time but begin to sit in the midst of it.

Looking for Benches

I accidentally discovered a feature on my phone that tells me various bits of factual information—today's date, the stock market numbers, what events are currently on my calendar, and what phone calls I missed today. As I scrolled through this newfound feature, I discovered a sentence at the very bottom: *You are now twelve minutes from home.* I haven't tested this out, but I'm guessing that wherever I am, this little feature will track how far I am from home, like a little fixed point I keep in my pocket.

Home is where you begin and to where you return.

The first bench we sit on is the one right outside our own doors, the one in the front of our apartment building, in the garden, in the backyard, in the grassy area of the cul-de-sac. These are the benches well worn from the sitting, from the watching, from the participating in the life where we are right now.

Our Tuesday bench is found wherever we call home. It's the room we face when we shut off the computer, the address we punch in to find out the distance between where we are and where we want to go, the place where we drape our clothes and our worries out for all to see.

Noticing, celebrating, and embracing our Tuesdays is an outward expression of an inward posture. Maybe if I practice noticing the small in my daily life I will come to identify with the small in my soul. Maybe small won't be something I fear or shrink from, but will be something I learn to embrace—slowly, quietly, with practice and intention.

And so we begin here, on our Tuesdays. But this is only a beginning. We don't stop at breathing in the moments. We use this practice to try on small, to uncover what else smallness has to teach us.

As I've been reading in the Gospels lately, I'm reminded of how personal, present, and local Jesus was when he was here on earth. He didn't teach about roads he hadn't traveled on or cultures he didn't live among (even though as all-knowing God, of course he could have). As Eugene Peterson points out in his book, *The Jesus Way*:

> Jesus did not work out his way of life in the intensely personal and God-oriented small towns of Capernaum, Chorazin, and Bethsaida simply because he didn't know any better, because that was the only world he knew. No, he *chose* them. He had equal access to Sepphoris and Tiberias and, over on the coast,

Caesarea, where the Herod way set the tone for how the people tended to live.[9]

He chose to sit with neighbors in neighborhoods, to walk with them in celebration and in grief, to eat meals and use the stuff of meals—bread, salt, wine, fish—in his conversations. He spoke of the future because that's why he came, but he didn't do so at the expense of the present. Jesus continued his life on earth the same way he started it—small, personal, and specific. He built metaphorical benches in the towns where he lived. Maybe he even built some literal ones.

Home Is *And*

> The discovery of God lies in the daily and the ordinary, not in the spectacular and the heroic. If we cannot find God in the routines of home and shop, then we will not find him at all. Ours is to be a symphonic piety in which all the activities of work and play and family and worship and sex and sleep are the holy habitats of the eternal.[10]
>
> —Richard Foster, *Prayer*

Maybe right now for you, home isn't a place, exactly. Maybe your home is a period of time or a group of people or one person in particular. Maybe home for you is a painful word, a lonely word, and a taunting, dangling carrot. Maybe you are living with your in-laws, your parents, or a gaggle of roommates. You are waiting for the next house, the next job, the next move, and the next something other than this.

Whether we live in a college dorm room or in a farmhouse on a hundred acres, we also live in the kingdom of God. And sometimes, home isn't what we expect it to be.

Unless you're driving to Wilmington or Charleston, there is no interstate that takes you directly to the coast of North or South Carolina. Instead, you have to take the back roads. This drive to the beach is always one I enjoy because the smaller towns offer vignettes of life you can watch as you drive by.

On the way to the beach during spring break, we passed a small, white house set away from the highway, driveway down one side with a field of yellow surrounding it. Those yellow fields were straight out of Oz, as if the poppies and the yellow brick road had a baby. I took a picture with my phone because of course I did.

While we were at the coast during our short spring break, I thought a lot about the place in life where we are now. We are currently living in a time of transition. After working as a youth pastor for twelve years, my husband, John, left that position to pursue a ministry opportunity that feels like a risk and an adventure. It's what we wanted and in many ways what we hoped it would be, but in my eagerness to leave the parts of the job that were taxing on my husband, I forgot to grieve leaving the parts that were good.

One of my own personal struggles is a temptation to always look ahead to the next thing, idealizing the other-ness of what is not rather than embracing the essence of what is. That's not always bad, but to be able to look ahead while also celebrating now is a delicate kind of art, to imagine what could be without discounting what is.

Once we got back home from our spring break trip, I looked up the yellow-brick-road, poppy-field house on Google maps because I wanted another glimpse of that beautiful yellow field. I found about where I thought it was on the highway and then switched to street view. With the wonder of modern day technology, a picture of that house popped up on my computer screen, as if I were standing on the road in front of it. There it was, the same lovely white house, but instead of a field of gold, it was surrounded by a field of brown, dry, and tired.

I suppose during the season when the Google robots came through to take the street view photos the flowers weren't in bloom. With a little research, I learn those yellow blooms are rapeseed blossoms. And they aren't just pretty flowers, they are also useful. When harvested, their seeds are one of the largest sources of the world's vegetable oil.

Maybe the woman who lives in that house looks forward to the rapeseed blooming every year, longing for what she knows will be even in the midst of what is. Maybe that field is the first thing she looks at when she walks outside no matter what time of year it is, remembering the beauty that was before and the promise of beauty to come again. Maybe "beauty" is a terrible word for what I'm trying to say here. Maybe she doesn't divide it up like that at all—the beautiful and the not beautiful. Maybe I don't get to say what's beautiful since I don't actually live there. Maybe those flowers are simply a way they make their living.

As a traveler with a curbside view, I notice her house because of all the pretty color, snap a photo and that's all I see. But it doesn't always look that way and the people who live there know that. They embrace the yellow when it comes but they don't leave along with it. They stay, they continue to live there, among the brown fields with their golden memory, beneath the sky when it's blue and when it's gray, within the little white house on the vast green lawn at the end of the gravel driveway.

Home isn't either beautiful or not, happy or sad, full or empty. Home is both. Home is *and*. Home has good parts, hard parts, marvelous and miracle parts. Home is where we celebrate and where we grieve, where we are hurt, broken and healed, and made whole again. And all of these parts are essential as we live in the kingdom of God.

I wish I could talk with the woman who lives in that house, to ask about the fields of gold in spring and how it feels in winter, about the distant tree line and living just off the highway and if she always has that "Fields of Gold" Sting song in her head.

More, I want to look at my own home the way I looked at hers. I want to see the rhythm of my life right now, to look for my own benches, and to see it all with eyes of a kingdom dweller, rather than eyes set on building my own city. I want to remember that small isn't always beautiful.

I want to remember the longing that comes from being human, to accept I won't always experience the satisfaction of that longing, but to understand how the longing informs my life and brings me gifts I may not even know to ask for. I want to remember how God set the longing for his kingdom in my heart and that when I settle for less than him, I'll always be homesick.

As it turns out, the journey to finding home is ongoing. I didn't expect it to be that way but it is. Yes, we have lived in our house now for seven years with no plans to move. Yes, I've lived in the same town for seventeen years. Yes, I feel like I've found a physical home, for now. But a home for our souls is a different thing and you can be settled and rooted in your house but be drifting in discontent in your soul. At least that's how it's been for me.

Our physical bodies may wander. At times our souls may feel orphaned and lost. But deep within, through the layers of external identity, we can burrow down to the deepest part of who we are, the quiet center we know is in there, the grounded place we've felt but can't see. This solid ground, this rock identity, this fixed point by which all other points are measured, this is our spiritual self, our alive-ness in Christ, our true home.

We long for home even while we have one, search for belonging even in the place where we belong. We don't get to pick our own small places. We take what's handed to us and decide what we're going to do with it. This is important work for body and soul: to settle in to my Tuesdays when I feel homeless, to look for a bench when I feel lost.

It's easier to celebrate in the beautiful small, but often it is in the terrible, the unexpected, and the uncomfortable small where we grow closer to Christ, share in his suffering, and ultimately find our true home.

As it turns out, a little more research on the golden flower yields this: "The rapeseed is a bright yellow flowering member of the *Brassicacea* family (mustard or cabbage family). It is a mustard crop grown primarily for its seed which yields about forty percent oil and a high-protein animal feed."[11]

The rapeseed is a mustard crop. *The kingdom of God is like a mustard seed.* The yellow kingdom of God, one inch above the ground, surrounds that little white house off Highway 38. The kingdom of God surrounds me too.

A Prayer for the Ordinary Aunties

We confess our disrespect for ordinary time. We recognize all the ways we despise it. But we long to see with kingdom-eyes the small ways you move in our Tuesdays. May we be people who see home right where we are, refusing to run into the future or pine over the past.

Gently poke our sleepy souls awake.

3

GATES & CUL-DE-SACS

Uncovering the Home We Bring with Us

> "Nowhere" is not the conjunction of no and where but, rather, the conjunction of Now and Here, which is actually Everywhere and is the only spot that we can truly experience God.
>
> —Brennan Manning, *Ruthless Trust*

The other day I was watching *The Brady Bunch* with my kids, the episode where Greg is a man now that he is a freshman in high school so he totally needs his own space. After much sweet-talking from Mrs. Brady, Mr. Brady reluctantly agrees to give up his den, the place where he does all his architecting, so Greg can have his precious space.

"Now, don't go and do anything drastic," Mr. Brady warns his man-child Greg. "No nail holes or paint on the wall." Oh Mr. Brady. How much you have to learn about home.

I used to be like Mr. Brady, thinking *drastic* meant a tiny hole in the wall. I cried real tears once trying to hang a picture. I realized it was crooked and I had to hammer another nail in the wall so the picture would be straight.

Real tears, I tell you. For the love.

The reason Mr. Brady and I felt so much anxiety about those pesky nail holes in the wall has little to do with the wall itself and everything to do with the perceived lack of control that those nail holes represent. I want to have dominion over the space I call home, right down to the tiny holes in the wall.

My sister has always influenced how I think about my home. Not only does she remind me that paint and nail holes are the least risky thing you could do in your life, but that home should be the safest place on earth to take a risk.[1] While I've grown in freedom at hammering nails into my walls, I've had to travel a more difficult path when it comes to accepting the transitions, struggles, and surprises that have come along the pathway of discovering my right-now home.

When Gates Become Cul-de-Sacs[2]

So, here we are. Living fully on this earth, within these walls painted Sea Salt and Alabaster White, among these people who look like us but who are also other-than us. While I think most would agree home is more than a house, it's also true that our lives play out in particular places at particular times. Here, not there. This city, not that one. These people, not those people.

The city of Greensboro, where I live, sits in the Piedmont region of central North Carolina, only an hour south of the Virginia border. If you drive an hour or so west, you'll be at the foothills of the Appalachian Mountains. A few more hours in the opposite direction is the grassy North Carolina coast. We aren't the biggest city in the state but we also aren't near the smallest. When those of us who live here are asked what's great about Greensboro, you'll often hear this common answer: *We're only a few hours from the mountains on one side and the beach on the other!*

On the one hand, it's nice to be so centrally located. But being close to nice places to visit doesn't seem to be a spectacular draw. *Come to Greensboro where you are only a few hours' drive from beautiful destinations!*

It sounds like I'm being negative, but history supports this commentary. In the mid 1800s, John Motely Morehead, the governor at the time, used his influence to ensure an east-west line of railroad tracks would travel through Greensboro, his hometown, rather than miles to the south as was planned. Years later, Greensboro became known as the Gate City because the busy train station located in the city was the actual gateway from one place to another.[3]

During college, that's what Greensboro was for me. Before I moved here at age twenty, I was in college in South Carolina and thought I was done living with my parents. They had recently moved from our home in Detroit to Greensboro, a town where I never planned to live. But I changed my major after my sophomore year which led to a college transfer to the University of North Carolina at Greensboro and a lack of income forced me to move back in.

Beneath the angst and the snobbery of my young adult independence, I harbored a quiet relief living at home again; to have someone cook for me, someone to help me with my laundry, someone to talk with over dinner. When 9:00 p.m. rolled around, Dad always got his second wind, announcing, "Anyone want some coffee?"

No one ever did, because who drinks caffeinated coffee at nine o'clock at night? I teased, but secretly I loved this nightly ritual. I went to bed knowing he was awake reading downstairs, the house smelling grown-up and familiar, the lamp from the living room leaving a whisper of light under my closed door as my body sank heavy into sleep.

I allowed myself to settle into living with my parents only because I knew it was temporary. Aside from a few students I met at school, I didn't know anyone in Greensboro. I was a serious student studying to become a sign language interpreter and once I had my degree, I knew I could go anywhere. Greensboro was a necessary stop on a long journey, a gateway to the rest of my life, a temporary pause on my way to the city.

As it turns out, my parents left Greensboro before I did. Dad got a job in Austin so he and Mom moved away, leaving me behind to finish my degree. And then I started to date John. Who not only *lived* in Greensboro but was actually born here too. His family lived here. He had roots. Two years later, we were engaged. When it was time to shop for a wedding dress, Mom and I found a simple strapless gown off the rack with buttons all the way down the back. I got the name of a seamstress from John's mom, who had lived in Greensboro for decades and seemed to know the right person to call for every leak, crack, and alteration. She gave me directions to her seamstress's house, and after piling my dress into the backseat of my car, off I went.

I followed the directions from my apartment off Pisgah Church Road closer in to the center of town. Carmella the seamstress lived in a quiet neighborhood with older houses surrounded by trees twice their size. After several turns and slow reading of street signs, I finally found her house on a quiet cul-de-sac, carried my dress inside to a bedroom in the front of the brown split-level, and made small talk as she worked to pin and pinch the candlelight fabric.

I was in a hurry that day, so I left my dress with Carmella in a rush to the next wedding-related errand. I had places to get to and things to do, as was to be expected.

I couldn't have known at the time that I had just pulled in to the cul-de-sac where John and I would raise our children. I couldn't have known I would one day move into the house two doors down from Carmella's brown split-level house, couldn't have known I would look at Carmella's house every morning when I woke up.

I thought Greensboro was my own gate city, a place to pass through on the way to the rest of my life. Except the rest of my life so far has happened right here in her midst.

Home often comes when we're waiting for the next big thing and finding home is often different from what we think it will be. We think we're looking for a gate to something more or something different, but instead we find ourselves in a cul-de-sac. Home often seems to show up on Tuesday mornings rather than on Saturday nights. While we stand on tiptoe looking ahead, home whispers, *Come sit for a while and take a breath. Perhaps you're already here.*

When Cul-de-Sacs Become Gates

I grew up in a small Indiana town where the world was about as big as a green backyard with a privacy fence, and here were her headlines:

Mama Cat Has New Litter of Kittens

Tire Swing Now Ready in Backyard

Happy Meal Has Strawberry Shortcake Prize

Beverly Cleary Writes New Book

Tornado Warning for Bartholomew County

Ten Speed Bike Spotted in Back of Shed—Birthday Coming Soon!

We lived in Columbus, Indiana, until I was eleven. Childhood ran without shoes in the alley behind the white house with the black trim, gravel hardening soft feet with every step, arms filled with Barbies, ears keen for the carnival sound of the ice cream truck, eyes filled with wonder. Back then it seemed nothing was ever going to change.

Grandma would live forever.

Sisters would always share rooms.

Saturdays would always mean donuts.

Dad would always hold beers.

Home would always be Gladstone Avenue.

In somewhat of a personal pilgrimage, I recently traveled back to Columbus alone. I imagined it might hurt to go back and remember, mostly because I can't re-create it. Still, I fly into Indianapolis, rent a car, and drive south down I-65 to Highway 31. Less than an hour later, I pull into town, both strange and familiar. I decide to navigate my way by memory to my old elementary school.

I think I'm going the right direction, but within minutes I realize I am headed out of town, straight into miles of cornfields, which, in Indiana, is easy to do.

I return to something familiar but still can't figure out the right way to go. It's strange to recognize everything but still not know where I am. Relenting, I pull out my phone and map out how to get to Smith Elementary School. I'm shocked as I watch the map draw the line from where I am to where I want to go. It is a very short line.

Four minutes.

Though I'm now a grown woman, I'm a kid again here. I never drove in this town, only rode in the backseat with occasional glances out the window. I knew landmarks, not street names. It's strange to feel a sense of home in a town where I'm now a stranger.

There was a time when Hoosier was my deepest identity. As a kid, I thought Indiana University's Bobby Knight was the best basketball coach in history, red and white were the only appropriate colors for a team, player Steve Alford was my secret boyfriend, and I actually believed their rival, Purdue, literally smelled bad. I had never been on their campus but what else could it smell like with initials like PU?

I felt a little sorry for the other people who lived in less important states and grieved when I became one of them in the summer of '88 when we moved to Iowa. I always thought Indiana was a cul-de-sac. Turns out it was a gate.

But today, I'm back in Columbus, driving to Smith Elementary School, on a mission. I have come back for reasons I'm not sure of, but they have something to do with wanting to remember something, to grab solid hold of my roots in a way that my last visit years ago didn't allow. I'm hoping that coming alone will help open me up to her stories, her history, and, in turn, my own.

I finally find Smith Elementary next to the cornfield right where I left her. I park in front of the school a little after four in the afternoon, pull around back wondering if the old playground is still there.

I'm thirty-seven years old, a person who has, for the most part, grown into her identity as a woman, a child of God, a wife, and mother. A woman who, as a girl, often felt as though perhaps I was missing a vital piece of myself, a particular piece that everyone else seemed to have. In many ways, I'm still coming to accept my Emily-ness, my own way of being in the world, my own okay-ness in the presence of God and others.

So I travel back to Columbus to understand a bit more of who I am, of how I am. To understand where my life began to perhaps shed light on where my life is now. I travel back realizing perhaps I'm still looking for that piece I think might be missing. I travel back to Columbus as one who both has a home but is looking for home at the same time.

Sitting in the parking lot of the school where I learned to read, I believe I make a hometown discovery—that home isn't somewhere out there, but somewhere *in here*. Maybe my trip to Columbus *was* about going back and remembering where I began, returning to the scene of the crime where the denying of my true self started. The front seat of a rental car became a bench for my soul as I looked out into the field behind my elementary school. I sat down on the inside with Christ, and there found home. Home was myself, hidden beneath the skin, the veins, the bone; tucked into the invisible place where God lives keeping company with me. In that small moment, I caught a glimpse of the kingdom of God.

Sometimes we think we're living in a cul-de-sac but really it's a gate. Other times we assume we're passing through a gate, but we end up circling a cul-de-sac. Either way, it's good to consider that home is a Person we bring with us rather than a destination we're trying to find.

The Importance of Looking Up

It's nearly dark so we grab our coats, head out to the grassy center of the cul-de-sac. It's the last day of February but the night is mild. Still, we need layers. We pile onto the benches, me with Ava and Stella on one, John and Luke on the other. We all tilt our heads back at the night sky. Luke picks up the iPad and lifts it above his head, using his space app to show us where the International Space Station is right now.

"It's behind Ms. Carmella's house," he says, looking straight ahead in the darkness.

I doubt we'll be able to see anything. Our cul-de-sac has a bright light near the basketball goal and all of our neighbors have their porch lights on. We see the moon and a few of the brightest stars, but even in our small city the lights beat out the stars every time.

"There it is!" John points to a spot low above Carmella's roof. "It's coming right over us."

Through bare branches of trees, a bright round star moves fast and steady. It swings in an arc right over our heads and we can't deny it now. It's hard to believe that tiny speck of light isn't a star but a football-field-sized space station, two hundred miles up, with people living and working outside of gravity or time. It's hard to believe because I can't see all the details. But science and the internet say it's true.

We stay outside until the tiny light sinks behind the trees on the other side of the cul-de-sac, delighted that we saw what we came here to see. The darkness comforts me tonight, whispers the relief small has to offer, pulls me down to the bench level to sit and find home. In this moment, a memory comes to mind and I'm nine years old again.

Mom and Dad pull my sister, Myquillyn, and me from our beds to drive out of town to the parking lot of our church, Shiloh Baptist, on State Road E 200 S. It's 1986. We anticipate a show because tonight we're going to see Halley's Comet.

It's cold but we brought blankets. They tell us this comet only comes around every seventy-five years or so and maybe one day when we're older, if we live long enough, we might get to see it again.

When we arrive at the church, I'm excited the way a kid mirrors the excitement of a parent, but I'm not sure I understand. As I stare up into the darkness, I wonder, where is the fireball traveling through the sky, a rainbow of color splashing out behind it? Where is the spectacle, the excitement? Tonight, all we see are stars, one maybe moving, maybe brighter than the rest, but I'm not sure.

But I'm nine and I want to pay attention because my parents seem to think this is important. Dad is even making us write a report about seeing Halley's Comet. It's not even for school, but of course I'll do it because it's Dad. I'm looking for a show but all I see is darkness.

Twenty-eight years later on my trip back to Columbus, I want to visit Shiloh Baptist Church but (shocker) I don't remember how to get there. I tap it into my phone. It says it's only ten minutes away. *That can't be right. The drive to church took forever when we were kids!*

A few turns and my phone tells me my destination is on the left. A half mile up the road, I see a familiar shape. There it is, slightly farther down the road than the phone can predict, but the shape is the same. The gray stone, the stained glass, the gravel drive. I wish I could go inside; wonder if the carpet is still orange. I pull into the parking lot, get out of the rental, and head toward the doors. One tug tells me what I already know. I won't be going inside today. Instead, I walk around to the side of the church to the spot where we watched Halley's Comet so many years ago.

Today I've already passed the age Dad was when they drove us out there to see the comet. I marvel at my parents' energy, to get two growing girls up in the night, to drive in the darkness to the church, to show us a comet that won't be back again in their lifetime. Why did they do it? What were they trying to teach us?

I understand now, at least more than I did then. This comet existed before me and will continue after me. I don't know why, but it feels important to acknowledge that, to notice what we can't control, even when it comes in the dark, even when it looks different than we thought, even when it seems ordinary.

It wasn't much to see from where we stood, but that's only because we were so far away. For even the smallest glimpse of this star-glory, we had to drive out of the city to see it and hunker down in the dark. The stars give me a good sense of my place in the universe. The small kind. The remembering kind. But the kind I can see whether I'm passing through a gate or living in a cul-de-sac if only I'm willing to look.

The kingdom of God is way up there, beyond the blackness of the night, above the stars and the moon. The kingdom of God is also now here, one inch above the ground, with us and within us. And home is wherever I am because Christ has made his home in me.

A Prayer for Those Standing at the Gates and Living in the Cul-de-Sacs

We confess our fear of trying new things, hard things, and scary things. We also recognize how we sometimes despise the idea of staying where we are. May we be open to discovering home right here instead of wishing for something different. May we release our tight-hold on *what could be* and be willing to sit on a bench in our front yard in the midst of *what is*. Be our courage and wisdom as we discern when to stay, when to move, and what it means to bring you with us.

Our Tuesday Home

Questions for Bench Dwellers

1. What kinds of things, situations, people, or circumstances cause you to feel small?

2. Have you ever seen the Milky Way?

3. How is your faith challenged differently during moments of crisis versus moments of ordinary time?

4. Have you ever unwrapped a Tuesday on purpose?

5. In what ways are you standing at a gate or living in a cul-de-sac?

6. What are some of your own hometown discoveries?

Part 2

Embracing
Our TUESDAY Work

More compassion. Less comparison.

Taking the easy yoke is to lay aside your projects or my projects, which are crushing—and this is where leaders come under intolerable pressure. It is because they are carrying their projects; they have presumed to take God's projects and made them their projects.

—Dallas Willard, *Living in Christ's Presence*

In this section you are invited to:

- stop dreading small beginnings and embrace the importance of your right-now work
- find the motivation to keep working even when you don't see results
- build a bench people want to sit on
- stay in your corner of the pool

EFFORT & OUTCOMES

The Truest Job Description
of Every Believer

Now faith is the assurance of things hoped for, the conviction of things not seen.

Hebrews 11:1

My dad used to watch our kids as toddlers and say under his breath, "We teach them when they're babies that they're the center of the world, and they spend the rest of their lives realizing they're not." It's true, we do it. We have to tend to them as though their world depends on it, because it does. They are so small. But so are we.

I spend a lot of time working hard to keep my world spinning around—craft the article, plan the meal, pick up groceries, deliver the brownies, write the email, ask him the questions, give them attention, and on it goes. We have to do these things, as they are our living, our livelihood, our art.

But our living and our art can quickly cross over into our obsessions and our burdens even as we will them not to. I don't want to live my life in such a hurry that I'm always closing the fridge door with my foot and scribbling out birthday cards in my car at the last minute. I want to make bread, or at least find the time to toast it.

As I begin to slow, I see smallness is not a punishment but a gift.

Rather than something to fear or run from, my smallness can be a celebration, an invitation for me to lie back on the wide, green earth and let the world spin the sun right up above me. I can breathe a sigh of sweet relief as I realize I had nothing to do with it. The effort is in believing that's true, not in controlling the outcome. I have to remember this. I must. When I don't, when I try to live big, I get tired.

It shows up in the smallest ways. For example, I'm out for the night with John, and my sister-in-law, Mercedes, has our kids. I text her and ask her to drop our girls off to swim at the pool with their friend. An hour later, I get a text from the pool friend's mom. *Are the girls coming to the pool? We haven't seen them yet.*

Frantic, I grab my phone. Why didn't Mercedes take them to the pool? Is something wrong?! But when I check my texting history, I realize I sent the first text to the wrong person and Mercedes never heard from me at all.

For a week I've been reading in the fifth chapter of the book of Mark, but today when I picked up my Bible and flipped to Mark, I couldn't find the passage where I left off yesterday.

Finally, after much flipping and turning of pages, I realize I've been reading in *Matthew*, not Mark. All week I thought it was Mark.

I go to strain the blueberries, the tiny kind that comes in a can in the muffin box, soaked in purple juice that needs pouring out. I grab the strainer and pour the blueberries right in. Only I'm not holding the strainer over the sink. Tipping the can to release the juice, I watch as the blueberries stop at the bottom of the strainer but the juice continues on, spilling all over my jeans, my shoes, the floor. For half a second I am confused. Why is juice everywhere?

My soul is jammed with so much activity that even the simplest things just aren't fitting in, like remembering a strainer has holes. Hurry has won the battle, has occupied the coveted land of my soul.

Deadlines do this to me. Big expectations in a small amount of time do this to me. Mainly lots of effort toward the wrong goals do this to me. I can feel the fast-moving world rush around me and within me. It's familiar but it's not welcome. In a fast-moving world, the small moments get trampled.

If I were a robot, I would need a re-boot. *Let's start this girl over; she's overheating.* I wonder if the Lord had that in mind when Jeremiah made his lamentation: "The Lord's loving-kindnesses indeed never cease, for his compassions never fail. They are new every morning; great is your faithfulness" (Lam. 3:22–23).

Effort is important, but I can't shake my fear of saying that. I hesitate to exalt effort because I know the tendency of my own soul to work hard to try to earn things I already have. Effort toward *excellence in my work* can silently morph into effort toward *perfection in my soul*. And before I can tease them apart my life becomes one defined by my failure and successes and I've forgotten who I really am. "Excellence" just becomes a more respectable word for "control," which is a fancy version of "manipulation," which is a physiological word for "sin," and did I really just align "excellence" with "sin"? Maybe I did. Maybe I meant to.

When I'm performing for my acceptance, burnout is always the result.

I don't see Jesus calling me to *excellence*. I do see him calling me to *himself*. And sometimes, on the kingdom of earth, moving close to Jesus looks like failure and embarrassment.

I've spent a lot of time thinking about what it means to do work well and in a healthy way without using my work as a way to define myself. Jesus says his load is easy and his burden is light, but he doesn't say there isn't a load or a burden. He recognizes there is something to carry but he invites us into the easy way of carrying it.

In my own life, I'm discovering that the subtle difference between my work feeling heavy and my work feeling light lies 100 percent on whether or not I'm holding on to the outcome of my work. When I trade all the effort I put into controlling outcomes with co-carrying the light, easy yoke of Christ, my small moments feel different.

What does "in Christ" effort look like versus "in Emily" effort? And how can I know the difference?

We Can Plant but We Can't Grow

How shall we picture the kingdom of God, or by what parable shall we present it? It is like a mustard seed, which, when sown upon the soil, though it is smaller than all the seeds that are

74

upon the soil, yet when it is sown, it grows up and becomes larger than all the garden plants and forms large branches; so that the birds of the air can nest under its shade. (Mark 4:30–32)

When I was younger, I had a necklace with a little glass pendant. Right in the middle of the pendant was a round, yellowish seed—a mustard seed. It reminded me of a poppy seed, the kind that came on the muffins Mom bought from the grocery store.

As I've read about Jesus's comparison of the kingdom of God to a mustard seed, I've learned some have challenged Jesus on this point, saying that, technically, smaller seeds than the mustard seed exist (the poppy seed, for example). But Jesus wasn't giving a lesson in plants or in gardening; he was teaching about his kingdom. And in doing so, he chose to use the things the people knew, comparing the seeds they actually planted in the place where they actually lived. He met them on their Tuesdays but cast a vision for the kingdom, one he was inviting them to be part of, one he was establishing within them and upon the earth.

It seems encouraging that Jesus compares the kingdom of God to a mustard seed. I want to grab on to my knowledge of what a mustard seed will become, starting small but growing big. I immediately look ahead to the outcome and forget to remember the small start.

What I didn't know before I started looking into it is also this: the mustard plant is actually kind of annoying. Though a mustard seed takes time to grow into a bush, it can sprout tiny green leaves in as little as three to four days if given the right conditions. They may not be fully mature, but the growth is still visible. In fact, the leaves can be used at this point in salads, sandwiches, and soups.[1]

A little more research uncovers this: "Mustard can easily become a garden pest because it self-sows readily. Don't plant in your most formal areas, and take care to harvest all the pods before the seeds scatter. Once the seeds drop to the ground, you'll have a tremendous weed problem that could take years to correct."[2]

This surprises me. I would have thought a seed Jesus compares to the kingdom of God would have better manners. Everything I read about the mustard plant says it grows easily and without much care. If you plant it in your garden, it can quickly take over. It grows where it is whether you want it to or not, stretches beyond the boundaries you set for it, unruly and untamed. If you look up a picture of a mustard plant, some images show it can grow taller than a man in all directions, shrubby and not particularly lovely.

The kingdom of God is like that?

When the kingdom of God takes root, it will grow without much human effort at all. What begins in secret will culminate in glory, we can be certain of that. What we can't be certain of is if the glory of this secret kind of growing will look like success in the eyes of the world.

We all have our pet peeves and we would probably all be a lot better off if we learned to keep them to ourselves. So I don't like spoons, big whoop. Nobody cares and I just sound weird when I admit it.

But some things we call pet peeves are more like deep, soul frustrations, the kind that make your neck splotchy hot and your heart speed up and your hands shake. The kind where you don't know if you want to tell someone off, cry in the corner, or move to a deserted island because people can be *the worst*.

One of those for me is what church people say when something happens that seems to catch on, to get big, or to grow.

I love watching what God is doing.

You obviously have found favor with God.

What a gift to see God's hand in this!

But when something happens that doesn't catch on, get big, or seem to be growing, we say things like this:

Maybe it wasn't God's will for you to try that after all.

Just wait, it will happen!

God's got this, just be patient.

Be patient for what? What is the measure of God's will or favor? Is it a number? Healthy things grow, but they may not grow at the rate, in the way, or in the timing I want. And the growth may be so small we never see visible progress in our lifetime, so messy that we may be tempted to prune back the branches, or so unexpected that we don't realize what God is doing because it looks so different than we thought it would.

Without realizing it (or maybe with full realization) we equate growth and size with God and favor, never stopping to consider the invisible kingdom we walk around in, the kind that starts as a mustard seed and grows whatever way it wants to, the kind that often works in secret, small ways—without our effort—like a seed, like yeast, like salt.

It's true, healthy things grow. That is good and natural. But let's explore what it feels like when all those efforts amount to, well, not much. What happens when our set goals aren't met and our brave dreams aren't realized? What happens when we believed it was the right thing, the right timing, the right call, and the right circumstances, but what was supposed to be the big finale was, instead, just a blip?

Does it mean we heard wrong? Moved too soon? Too late? Could we have done more?

These are the kinds of questions we can't really answer, not with certainty anyway. All we can do is build the benches we believe God has for us, to bend down low to the earth around those benches and plant seeds we hope will sprout, and then remember how true it is that we can plant but we can't grow. May this be a relief and not a burden as we release the outcomes into the capable hands of God.

We Can Act but We Can't Determine

Looking over some writing I did a few years ago, I read these words: *We are not called to action. We are called to belief.*

I now see a lot of problems with that statement.

In the context of the piece, I get it. For a recovering good girl, I am a woman who has spent a lot of life finding my identity and acceptance in my ability to perform well. So when it comes to acceptance before God, we are not called to the kind of effort and action that tries to earn our own worthiness and love. We are invited to believe we have those gifts already.

But belief expresses itself through action, so for me now that statement I made is misleading. It isn't one or the other. *It's both.* I have been learning about the effort it actually takes believers to believe. I say I'm a believer but then when I'm offended, hurt, embarrassed, or insulted, my biggest belief is in myself and my own opinions and defenses.

The belief is in the verbs. Hope. Persevere. Feed. Help. Listen. True belief is movement toward God even in the midst of confusion or frustration or fear.

The Lord told Moses to stretch out his hands over the sea and up came the walls of water. But Moses had to act on his belief.

The lame man had to pick up his mat and walk.
The bleeding woman had to reach out her hand to touch.
Noah built.
The disciples followed.
Esther asked.
Abraham went.

And what more shall I say? For time will fail me if I tell of Gideon, Barak, Samson, Jephthah, of David and Samuel and the prophets, who by faith conquered kingdoms, performed acts of righteousness, obtained promises, shut the mouths of lions, quenched the power of fire, escaped the edge of the sword, from weakness were made strong, became mighty in war, put foreign armies to flight. (Heb. 11:32–34)

None of these people moved perfectly, but faith is fully expressed when we bring our imperfect work into the presence of God and move toward others in love. We are not under *pressure* to act. We have been set *free* to act, to move, to make choices, to live out what we say we believe.

Learning how to listen *and then move*, how to consider *and then choose* is an important journey I'm still walking. But I can't forget the effort it takes to create *and then release*. I need a daily reminder to let go of outcomes, to remember I can plant seeds but I can't make them grow, I can create art but I can't make it sell, I can act in faith but I can't determine the outcome.

Jesus taught his disciples to pray today for daily bread, the kind we can't carry into tomorrow. Looking to the future may give meaning to my work, but I have to be careful not to look to the future to find meaning for my *life*. There is a daily-ness to my work, a small-moment perspective that whispers for me to connect with the work in my right-now hands, not because it's going to become something Big and Important, but because Someone who is Big and Important is here, with me, in me, today. I can exert the effort and risk of moving, choosing, and releasing because he is with me and the outcome rests safely in his hands.

We Can Build It but We Can't Fill It

> To be in the yoke with Christ is to pull his load with him. What is his load? It is to bring the reign of God into ordinary human life. That is why he came the way he did, lived the way he did and died the way he did. In the midst of a world of ordinary human life. That was his message. And his message was to everyone.[3]
>
> —Dallas Willard

Sometimes I feel like I'm walking through a battlefield and my enemy is an army of numbers. How many people showed up to that group we started? How many units of that product sold? How many shares did I get on that photo? How much money did I make last week, month, year?

In my work, I admit it hurts to be small. When I've spent *weeks* writing, cutting, pasting, revising, and editing something, it's discouraging when I share it and only receive a handful of responses. Especially when I get on Twitter and see one of my peers launch a product that has twenty-five thousand sign-ups in less than twenty-four hours. I know it doesn't matter. I know this. I know these numbers don't define me. But sometimes I feel like I'm fighting my way through an army of numbers and there is no indication they plan to surrender.

I've tried to fight numbers with effort. It never works.

I have a friend who is one of the most prayerful people I know in real life. She doesn't just say she'll pray about something. When she tells me she'll pray for me, I know for sure it's true. One of the words I think of when she comes to mind is *faithful*.

She and I are planning a gathering, and the other day she asked me how many I thought would come. I gave her a number and she responded that she is praying for a much higher number than the one I said. I had to laugh. I don't pray for numbers. Not because I think it's wrong to do so, but more because I just get weird about it in my own head. "If you build it, they will come" isn't from the Bible but a quote (actually a misquote)[4] from the movie *Field of Dreams*. I have built many things and "they" have not come.

Once I prayed for three hundred people to show up to an event we had planned. We had less than fifty. Another time I asked God how much money I should donate to a cause. Ten different numbers bounced through my mind until I just had to pick one because the continual battle to try to figure out which number would be the *best* was giving me a headache.

I have never been a person to whom God sees fit to give a particular number. I know people with whom he does speak that way. *We needed $151.23 and we got that exact amount in the mail from an anonymous giver!* I love those kinds of stories and am thankful to hear them. I'm simply not a person who has ever received or written a check like that, not that I know of. God doesn't speak to me that way, or at least he hasn't yet.

Instead of focusing on the numerical outcomes of the work I do every day, it helps me to consider some other numbers.

Five thousand. To sit on a bench with my work means to keep company with a small boy who had a small lunch that fed five thousand men. My part is not feeding five thousand men. My part is giving my lunch to Jesus.

Twenty-one. To sit on a bench means to keep company with David, who was anointed by Samuel twenty-one years before he was appointed king over all of Israel. My part is not to rush to vocational outcomes. My part is to wait in the presence of God.

One. To sit on a bench means to keep company with one young girl before a glorious angel, sent by God to invite her into the greatest mystery of all time. *You will bear a child and call his name Immanuel.* And her one small yes became the holy gateway from heaven to earth. Our part is not ushering heaven to earth. Our part is one small yes.

Too many to count. To sit on a bench is to keep company with Abraham who, along with Sarah, tried to control the promise God made of an heir. But God told him it wouldn't happen by Abraham's own effort or planning. Instead, he "took him outside and said, 'Now look toward the heavens, and count the stars, if you are able to count them.' And he said to him, 'So shall your descendants be'" (Gen. 15:5). Our part is not making the promise come true. Our part is to count the stars.

Heaven is already here. With our work, we get to build benches that line the roads of the kingdom of God. But we don't get to say how many will sit on them.

We Can Offer but We Can't Control

John and I had been married only a year when we went with a group of middle school students to a summer camp in 2002.

The speaker was well known and super cool and the worship band led high-energy songs. It all built to a crescendo toward the end, the worship speaker shouting, "Let's see you kids out-worship your leaders!"

I wanted to throw up. I sat in my seat, sick with lights and the pink smoke, sick to have all the kids raising their hands and jumping to the beat—not because it was wrong for them to do that, but because they seemed to be doing it because it's what the person with the microphone told them to do. He built a bench with his music but he was forcing people to sit on it the way he thought they should.

One of our students—high ponytail, huge grin, white T-shirt—grabbed me by the arm and said, "Come on! Jump!" And I refused. She pulled and I sat heavier and said no.

If that happened today, I probably would have handled it with a little more grace. But I was devastated by the manipulation happening right in front of me, angry over the blatant lack of grace in that room because it seemed like they were saying that if you love God then of course it will look this particular way.

There was no respect for anyone's individual experience of God, no room to consider perhaps this isn't how everyone worships. There was only one way, and it wasn't necessarily the way of Jesus, it was the way of the stage.

I remember how her small fingers had gripped my wrist, and I cringe because in a flash in my imagination, we trade places. I wonder how many times I have been the one in the white T-shirt and ponytail with my fingers gripped around the wrist of another. How many times have I been the one trying to pull people up from their seat to convince them to worship and experience God my way?

I know the truth of the gospel, I know God is with me, I know his Spirit works in my life.

I also know God has many faces and I don't always understand the ways he may choose to show himself. I know how he has spoken to and moved within me. I do not know how he might speak to or move within someone else. I can only partner with Christ, listen, walk, and believe. I can only be with him, be loved by him, and be with and love others. I can't control their behavior.

This is all I can do. This is my only job. This is my truest job description.

I can build a bench and send out an offering, but I can't make people come and I can't force them to sit. I can show up on Tuesday, sit on my bench, and lean into my smallness in the presence of Christ.

This kind of small isn't the kind we dread, it's the kind we hope for.

It isn't being crushed beneath the weight of something bigger, it's being held up by the strength of God's love.

It's an invitation to home, both the physical home where I live right now and the spiritual home Christ is for me. And I am for him, too.

I want to say embracing smallness will lead to big impact, grand endings, and the very best outcomes. It will, if your impact is Christ. If your ending is Christ. If the outcome is Christ.

We were made to build, to co-create, to bring glory to God with the work of our hands, to move into the world as unique reflections of Christ. But we were *not* made to fill rooms, stadiums, or bank accounts. We were not made to fill our souls with worth we construct with our hands.

We plant, trusting God for the growth.

We act in faith, trusting God for the outcome.

We build, trusting God to fill.

We offer, trusting God with the response.

We remember the mustard seed that is like the kingdom of God, the seed that will grow anywhere and everywhere even without our help. We remember this is a "hardy seed that remains viable for years—even centuries."[5]

As I'm driving around Greensboro in the middle of October, beneath the canopy of trees declaring glory, I'm amazed at how silent they are about it. I'm thankful we have a God who sometimes chooses to tell his big story in small, delightful, quiet ways.

A Prayer for the Bench Builders

When it comes to our work, we confess our desire to grow, determine, fill, and control. Remind us these outcomes belong to you. Instead, may we simply plant, act, build, and offer, releasing the outcomes into your hands because they are not our business. Continue to be yourself in us as we dive into places where we can't measure results. We want your presence to be its own reward. Be our kind companion as we build our benches so we may be kind companions for those who come to sit.

SUCCESS & ENVY

Accepting the Importance of Our Right-Now Work

> Somewhere deep in our hearts we already know that success, fame, influence, power, and money do not give us the inner joy and peace we crave.
>
> —Henri Nouwen, *The Selfless Way of Christ*

After twenty years of working in the academic world—Yale, Harvard, and Notre Dame—priest Henri Nouwen began to sense within himself what he called "a deep inner threat."

"Everyone was saying that I was doing really well, but something inside was telling me that my success was putting my own soul in danger." He recognized within himself a deep loneliness and darkness he couldn't seem to shake, which led him to ask God for direction.

God's answer came to him in the form of a person. He met Jean Vanier, the founder of the L'Arche communities for people with intellectual disabilities. Nouwen says God told him to "go and live among the poor in spirit and they will heal you."

"So I moved from Harvard to L'Arche, from the best and the brightest, wanting to rule the world, to men and women who had few or no words and were considered, at best, marginal to the needs of our society. It was a very hard and painful move, and I am still in the process of making it."

I think about Henri Nouwen's transition from the large, influential life to a small, hidden one. He said it was the unlikely way God chose to save him from spiritual burnout.[1] It's counterintuitive to think that success could be the doorway to burnout. No one sets out to fail. In his situation, it seems it would have been easy for Nouwen to sink into the trap of comparison, measuring the seemingly unimportant work in front of him with the respectable academic work of his contemporaries.

In my own life, I recognize my tendency to look over at the work of others rather than down at the work in front of me.

Finding True Success in Our Eight-Foot Assignments

No matter how much I wish they didn't, my children love to go to the indoor water park. If you live in a part of the world where the weather is warm year-round, then you may not understand the need for such parks. But here in North Carolina where pools close for half the year, the indoor water park is a relief for many. But not for me. I can't think of a worse invention on planet Earth. *I have an idea! Let's build a bunch of slides in a huge, dark-ish gymnasium. Then let's crank the heat up to 275 degrees and add lots and lots of chemical water.*

For hour upon endless hour, we walk around in our bathing suits without even the perks that bathing suits usually offer. You can't get a tan because you're inside. You aren't motivated to cool off because it's the middle of winter and you've been cold for three months. Not only that, but you've just realized your suit is super snug because the last time you wore it was August and now it's the middle of winter and, *Oh yeah, I have skin* and *Oh no, it's white like paste.*

The first time we went to one such place, I was all geared up for what they call "fun"—wore my suit, sported my whiteness, braved the Totem Towers. But halfway through standing in line on wet steps with my shivering children, I realized I was miserable.

As I tried to angle myself into the railing (both to have some kind of covering from my line-mates behind me as well as to protect my frontal area from the giant bucket of water that emptied itself every sixty seconds), I caught a glimpse of the chair section over to my right.

That's right, the chair section. Row upon endless row of lounge chairs. That's when I realized I was doing this wrong. The secret to the indoor water park that more experienced mothers obviously already knew is this: *don't wear your bathing suit to the water park.*

It sounds lame, I know. But this might be one of those times when it is appropriate to pull out the whole *I carried you for nine months inside of me so now Daddy has to take you down the water slide* card.

And so, on our second visit to Water Torture Park I came armed with my newfound wisdom in the form of a cozy novel and a pair of long pants. Even though it was 275 degrees with air thicker than a Low Country summer, I managed to enjoy myself. As it turns out, I couldn't focus on my book because there was too much going on, too many people to watch. The most fascinating among them were the lifeguards.

For all the ways the indoor water park disappointed me, the lifeguards nearly made up for it. These were no whistle-twirling, chair-lounging, teenage-flirting type of lifeguards. These people were serious and focused.

First, there were a ton of them. Second, they each had a whistle in their mouths—Popeye style—and an orange life raft tucked under their arm at all times. But the most compelling thing about these lifeguards was the fact that they were not only always on their feet, *they never stopped moving.*

It was as if they were each assigned an eight-foot length of the pool, no more and no less. They were responsible for those eight feet and anyone who swam within them. They paced their assigned distance back and forth at the edge of the pool, eyes never leaving the water. It was impressive to watch, as much as I didn't like admitting that *anything* impressed me at the water park.

Their job wasn't to watch the whole pool, only their assigned area. Besides, there were ten more lifeguards spaced out perfectly around the pool, each doing their job, responsible for their small section. They weren't constantly looking over at the other lifeguards to make sure they were doing their part. They weren't hyperventilating over the parts of the pool that weren't their responsibility.

They only watched a simple eight feet.

Those lifeguards taught me a valuable lesson about my own calling. I can get super inspired and motivated to do Big and Important Things, and when I'm in that place, the possibilities seem endless. But possibility can be as overwhelming as it is inspiring. At first it can feel terribly exciting to imagine anything is possible. That is, until I sprint flat into the wall of my own limits in the form of lack of time, lack of energy, comparison, competition, and distraction.

Could it be possible we have it wrong? Maybe success isn't in believing I can do anything but in knowing I can do nothing. My limits—those things I wish were different about myself—are perhaps not holding me back but are pointing me forward to pay attention to my small, eight-foot assignment.

It seems to me when I finally recognize my inability is when Christ shows up *able* within me. But he doesn't equip me to do every job possible, he equips me to do the job meant for me.

If you're willing to face your inability, you might see something you desperately need to continue—your limits can be a gift, showing you what is outside your circle of influence and responsibility so that you may embrace and focus on the small part that belongs to you and *only* to you. It's possible that the reason we are so overwhelmed is because we are focused on the whole pool, forgetting our eight-foot assignment.

As I watched those lifeguards, a phrase my dad often says came to mind—*You just focus on your corner of the pool.* I know what he means now: you have a job to do and it doesn't look like mine or his or theirs. It looks like yours. It isn't the whole pool, but it's important. The fact that you can't cover the whole pool at once doesn't mean you are a failure, it just means you have the wrong goal. It also means you need other people around you to do their job too. Success means recognizing which part belongs to me as I depend on Christ and which parts belong to others.[2]

The best way to sabotage my own success is to be obsessed with someone else's. Instead, I want to focus on the benches in my own front yard, the ones I call home as well as the ones I'm being asked to build. They won't look like the benches in someone else's yard, and that's precisely the point.

The Success of Weakness

Brennan Manning told the story of a time when he filled in as a speaker at a conference in Vail, Colorado, in place of someone who had to drop out last minute. His reason for saying yes to the invitation? "I wanted to be identified with the superstars on the circuit. Hungry for approval and acceptance, I saw Vail as a venue to glory."[3]

At that same time, Fil Anderson was living here in Greensboro, working as the regional director of Young Life. His busy schedule left little room for a personal retreat, but he headed to this same conference in Vail anyway, desperate for some kind of relief from his frenetic lifestyle.

During the conference downtime, Fil signed up to meet with one of the speakers for a session in spiritual direction. The speaker's name? Brennan Manning.

Brennan described the meeting like this: "So two desperately insecure men, total strangers to each other, showed up in Vail . . . My door was open, Fil popped in, and one of the few deep friendships I have ever had in my life began that sunlit morning."[4]

Fil is a family friend of ours, though I didn't know him back in those days when he was running on empty. Last November, I heard Fil tell this story, of meeting Brennan and coming to the end of himself, a story made even more powerful since Brennan's passing in April 2013.

Two men, both looking for some kind of glory, both wanting to find significance and hope in something. Brennan admitted he went to that conference with twisty motives—glory, recognition, significance. Fil admitted he signed up to meet with Brennan because he wanted his autograph.

Two insecure, imperfect men, limping together into the presence of God. Yet both moving, *at least moving*, toward that hope even with all their inconsistencies and imperfections. They didn't move perfectly—motives weren't clear, calendars weren't ready, lives weren't ordered. I would even venture a guess that both Brennan and Fil despised the way they tried to cling to glory even though they knew better.

But once they got together, the Holy Spirit met them, had compassion for them, and offered his presence to them in the form of one another. At some point, either during their meeting that day or another meeting later, Brennan gave Fil these verses from Matthew 11:28–30, from *The Message*:

> Are you tired? Worn out? Burned out on religion? Come to me. Get away with me and you'll recover your life. I'll show you how to take a real rest. Walk with me and work with me—watch how I do it. Learn the unforced rhythms of grace. I won't lay anything heavy or ill-fitting on you. Keep company with me and you'll learn to live freely and lightly.

After he read these verses, Brennan offered Fil this simple instruction: "Sit with these words until they become the truest thing about you."

When I'm looking sideways over at the success of others or longing to have or be something I have not or am not, these Matthew 11 words are not the truest thing about me, at least not in my experience. But I know this kind of rest, this kind of love, this kind of *knowing* has the potential to change everything.

Jesus doesn't say, *Come to me, keep company with me, and you'll learn to do nothing, to be passive, to never work again.* He says, *Keep company with me and you'll learn to live freely and lightly.* Being with Jesus brings a different kind of living and a different kind of working—the kind that starts with being.

I'm so glad these two men showed up that day in Vail, Colorado. I don't even care that their motives were wonky. All that matters is that they showed up willing.

And the Spirit of God spoke through Brennan to Fil.

And then, through Fil to me.

And now, maybe, to you.

For Better or for Worse

Celebrating our smallness in the midst of our Tuesday moments looks surprisingly similar in failure as it does in success.

Let's say you finally land the interview for the job after much preparation. You know you are one of only three candidates out of a pool of five hundred. You find just the right clothes to represent your inward confidence—or rather to camouflage the fact that you have none. You show up as you are with what you have to offer. You wait for days to hear back, and then the call you hoped for comes.

You get the job. You are picked, chosen, the one they have been looking for. What does it mean to celebrate smallness here?

Small says take the job with joy and confidence. You have been given your eight-foot assignment. Take it, but remember it doesn't define you.

What if you do all this—same suit, same confidence—but they pick someone else? What does it mean to celebrate smallness when things don't turn out as you hoped?

You grieve, you struggle, you feel the disappointment. To be small in the midst of disappointment simply means to be open to the presence of Christ with what is true right now, to remember you aren't alone, and to keep company with your weakness.

You have been given your eight-foot assignment. Take it, but remember it doesn't define you.

I can celebrate my smallness in success and in failure, in inspiration and in disappointment, in excitement and in boredom, in confidence and insecurity. This is my Tuesday job, my eight-foot assignment. Celebrating my smallness in the midst of failure and success is important, kingdom-building work.

Instead of a fearful place I have to either defend or run from, small can become my new home. Small can become hilariously delightful, fun, and free. I can come with little things to offer, with no agenda, with the day as it is and not as I wish it were instead. I'm small, and this is as it should be.

True smallness is an invitation to live as I was meant to live, to accept my humanity, and to offer my ability and my inability, my sin and my success, my messes and my masterpieces into the hands of God.

When It Feels Like My Personality Gets in the Way of My Success

Lately I've been noticing I'm taking even longer than usual to process events and experiences, requiring broader margins and more white space to consider their impact and my desire. I am a hard worker who meets deadlines and can usually finish tasks when they need finishing. I am also a slow processor who has to allow conversations, ideas, and other influences to marinate before I can grab hold of them. These two true statements fight.

What is good for my inner health is often frustrating for my work.

I haven't always been accepting of this pace. I have tried to discipline the slow out of me. I've read blog posts and books on how to be productive, how to write even faster, and how to do other things I'm not naturally great at. As I mentioned before, I have learned to do more in less amount of time, to focus in less than ideal situations, to finish, ship, and deliver. But it doesn't come natural for me. I find myself envious of those who seem to consistently organize, produce, and share. They make it look so easy.

Productivity skills have helped me meet important deadlines and release unnecessary perfectionism.

The problems come when I foolishly try to apply these same skills to my inner life.

The soul and the schedule don't follow the same rules.

The truth is my slowness is not a fault or a sin, but fighting it might be. I tend to think my limitations are my burdens but perhaps they are actually my gifts if I'm willing to see them that way.

Because once I finally grab hold, I will take the conversation, the idea, and the influence all the way in, allow it all to move and shape my thoughts and my actions. These slow-cooked thoughts will influence how I love, how I think, how I write. They will fill up holes of misunderstanding, smoothing some of the rounded question marks into straight-up exclamation points.

As much as I sometimes wish I could post a bulletin to this fast-moving world, announcing a celestial time-out, I know that isn't the answer. Many people are in a season of speed, a time of movement, of action, and go. But that is not where I usually am. And I cannot wait for the world to stop to embrace my permission for slow.

What part of your personality seems to fight against your own perceived ability to succeed? What might happen if you stopped bullying your personality into submission and instead began to welcome it as a kind friend?

So here's to you, my fellow slow-processors. Take the long way home. Embrace the silence to consider. Give yourself permission to think, to listen, to be sure.

Here's to waiting before we move, pausing before we speak, and taking a week to cross off everything on our day list.

Here's to trusting that we are made on purpose and that our natural hesitations may be our greatest gifts rather than our liabilities. Here's to believing we have something to offer but that doesn't mean we have to offer it in the ways the world tells us we must.

Here's to giving ourselves permission to bring our gifts into the presence of God, knowing he will bring them out of us in his own timing and in his own way.

Here's to remembering our job isn't to manufacture success.

Here's to seeing the work of our peers, our sisters, our brothers, and our co-workers and celebrating their accomplishments, awards, and beauty.

Here's to knowing their success does not take one thing away from us.

Here's to moving when we sense God moving, and listening when he says to stop talking.

Here's to shuffling our feet, playing on the floor, and staring out the window if we need to.

Here's to listening to our questions, sitting in the darkness, and letting our experiences do their deep work within us.

Here's to a long, deep breath.

And here's to not letting our slowness boss us. Embrace it and learn it, but don't let it force perfection. Let slow do what slow does best: nourish, strengthen, and hold.

Here's to deep roots, strong ties, and slow art.

A Prayer for the Right-Now Workers

We confess our tendency to look for our identity in every face but yours. We long to know how we measure up compared to someone else. Take our comparison and give us compassion, for others as well as for ourselves. Reveal to us our eight-foot assignments and remind us that we aren't responsible to control the world, only to bring the cares of those eight feet into your capable hands. Help us to embrace the shape of our own design, being ever mindful that you have made us as we are even as we are being transformed into your likeness. May we stop trying to wring out our own brand of humanity. Rather may we trust you to show yourself through our unique personalities.

6

STAIRWELLS & STAGES

Learning to Receive the Gift of Obscurity

O little town of Bethlehem . . . Kingdom comes to places like you.

—Ann Voskamp, *The Greatest Gift*

Every year in the middle of May, America chooses an idol. I've watched *American Idol* over the years and am fascinated with the entire process.

The way I understand it, the process begins during the summer when people between the ages of fifteen and twenty-eight trek to an audition city near them to sing for a group of judges. The idea is to find an obscure, no-name person doing a somewhat thankless job—waitress, pawn shop worker, student, father—who also happens to have a killer voice. They are then plucked out of obscurity and placed on a stage for the world.

If they make it through the first round, they sing for producers. Then if they really truly can sing (or if they're so bad as to be entertaining), they get to eventually audition for the celebrity judges. This is the part they show on television. At this point, they will either get a "ticket to Hollywood" for the next round of competition or they're out.

It continues on this way week after week, the judges narrowing the field each round, until finally they get the group down to ten or twelve who will perform for America's votes. They sing, the viewers call in or vote online, and the person with the least amount of votes goes home. The process continues until they are left with two in the finale and then, finally, just one American Idol.

As the contestants progress each week, those who stay in the competition say things like, *Anything is possible! Just follow your dreams!* And the losers, especially the ones who leave early in the process, tend to say things like, *No one wanted this more than I did*. But that isn't true because they all want it equally.

The experience of the winner is that anything *is* possible. The experience of the non-winner is profound disappointment. But the big picture truth is anything isn't possible and also, a lot of people wanted it the same amount. It's an accurate picture of desire and disappointment literally played out onstage.

Our Souls Aren't Made for Fame

On the night of May 23, 2012, I watched as the final two contestants, Jessica Sanchez and Phillip Phillips, stood center stage as host Ryan Seacrest called for the lights to dim and prepared to read the final results. As he read the winner's name, an interesting thing happened.

Winner Phillip Phillips didn't jump up and down, fall on his knees in victory, or make number one signs at the camera. Most of the winners of this show don't, in fact. He didn't scream into the camera or showboat for the crowd. He was almost nearly silent and still. For a guy with a name important enough to be used twice, this seems especially humble.

It had been a long five months of competition, reportedly made even more difficult for Phillip specifically because of problems he had been having with his health. As a viewer watching from home, I thought he looked relieved. Not that he had won, but that it was over.

As is tradition, a guitar materialized, music started, and Phillip was expected to sing a vocal victory lap for the crowd. He made it through the first verse and chorus, but by the time the second verse started he was finished, the emotion and exhaustion fully caught up. He surrendered to it, lowered his head, and let the background singers take over.

As the sparks shot out from the screen behind him and the confetti began to drop all around him, he didn't seem able to take it in. A phrase went through my mind I had once heard counselor Al Andrews say in an interview: *The human soul was not made for fame.*

Deep down, we know this. Deep down we long for solid and for true and we know earthly fame is all airy lights and flashing bulbs and the stuff of grasping but never quite getting. But sometimes we still pine for attention and recognition, for the bright lights and fancy nights in all their various forms. We still desire to be exalted or even just be near to those who are.

As Phillip stood there on the Idol stage, overwhelmed with his own success and attention, it was like his soul was turning inside out and he didn't know how to handle it. When he started to cry, all he could do was walk off the stage, his head still down, straight into the arms of his waiting family on the front row. I can't pretend to know what was going on in his mind, but as the music continued without his lead voice, none of the glitz seemed to matter. His family opened wide their arms to him and he disappeared into them, like he was hiding in the comfort of his own smallness. The crowd and the cameras crammed importance into him by the truckload, but it seemed he didn't want to receive it, couldn't receive it, didn't know how.

We hear all the time one unfortunately common result of this fame-cram. I saw a glimpse of Boy George on the news the other day. He's older now, but at the age of twenty-one, his band The Culture Club became instantly famous with the successful release of their single *Do You Really Want to Hurt Me*. The newscaster told his story in the voice-over and said this line: "The instant stardom of Boy George led him to a drug and heroin addiction."

If our souls were made for fame, wouldn't we more often hear statements like, "Her instant stardom led her to a life of peace, joy, and happiness." But we never hear that. In fact, the ones who have managed to remain healthy in the spotlight seem to be those who most downplay their own fame, those who have relationships to keep them grounded; not the ones who bask, revel, and delight in their fame, but the ones who continue to do their work in spite of it. Only a fool opens up his arms, tilts back his head to the heavens, and takes it all in, declaring to be king of the world.

The televised talent shows are a fascinating study of how we mill about here on earth, putting our stars on certain people, lifting them up when they seem to be the underdog and then tearing them down when they get too big. They share their art and we want to hear it, but soon, if they are too successful or get too much attention, they become the object of our narrowed eyes and pointy fingers. *If we can't win, then neither can they.*

Beth Moore says this about the danger of adoration: "I've learned along the way that to the height a person idolizes you, he/she can despise you. A switch flips and adoration turns to hatred. Never feed someone's out-of-kilter adoration. Mutual respect, affirmation, and gratitude are beautiful. Godly. Adoration can turn deadly. I have never once had a person turn out to be dangerous or disturbing and vicious who wasn't an over-the-top 'fan' first."[1]

We do it with our athletes and our movie stars and our "professional" Christians too. We know better than to worship them, but we put them up slightly higher than ordinary. We forget (or maybe we never really understood) that Christ holds all things together and all things were created for him and through him. He is the firstborn over all creation (see Col. 1).

We are made to worship. And we're so good at it. Pay attention at any concert you attend and watch the faces of those closest to the stage. On the late night talk shows, listen to how loudly the audience laughs at the mediocre jokes of the celebrity guest. Count the number of famous faces on the magazines in the checkout aisle. Wait in line after the game with the fans of the team. Watch how patient they are to meet the quarterback.

I stood behind Katie Holmes once in an airport Starbucks and, when I realized it was her, proceeded to follow-slash-stalk her to her gate. We saw Daniel Stern, the actor who played the tall bad guy from *Home Alone*, in the lobby of a New York City hotel once and nearly tripped over ourselves pointing at him. Taye Diggs followed me on Twitter and I didn't even care that he follows 273,000 other people or that the people who run his social media account are either grossly misinformed about who I am or that they followed me by accident because . . . Taye Diggs!

You probably have your own celebrity sighting stories to tell. I'm not saying being a fan is bad, I'm saying it's *natural*.

And while of course we would never say that we worship these celebrities, these examples are shadows pointing to a greater reality. As John Ortberg so simply points out in his book *Soul Keeping*, "The soul must orbit around something other than itself—something it can worship. It's the nature of the soul to need."[2] Worship is woven into our design. But our souls were not made for this kind of earthly fame—either to receive it or to give it to each other.

Most of us will never have the kind of fame status that would cause someone to recognize us in an airport. But there is another kind of fame we often long for, the kind where we get recognized in our church for the work we do or praise in our own families. There's still fame to be had in our own hometowns.

When John and I got engaged, he was in seminary getting his Masters of Divinity in pastoral studies. From the very beginning of our relationship, I knew my life would be characterized to some degree by being married to a pastor.

Once he graduated, he got a job working in youth ministry right before our wedding. For the next twelve years, he served as a youth pastor. Six of those years were spent with about eighty middle school students in a church of fifteen hundred, and the last six were spent with hundreds of high school students in a church of over five thousand. He took the trips, led the studies, planned the games, taught the lessons, scheduled the concerts, met with the parents, baptized the believers, prayed with the doubters. He celebrated the graduates, grieved with the dying, and sat with those they left behind. A lot of families in Greensboro have been impacted by John's ministry over the years.

It's a regular job in a regular-sized town, but there's a certain amount of respect that comes with being a pastor. The same can be said for teachers, doctors, counselors, and any number of other positions. There is a tendency to categorize people based upon their position among us and shine the spotlight of human recognition, applause, status, and reputation on them or hope it gets pointed toward us.

I once heard author, speaker, and anti–human-trafficking activist Christine Caine say this: "If the light that is within you isn't brighter than the light that is upon you, the light that is upon you will kill you. The gift that is in you will destroy you unless you have a faith that can sustain you."

Who could say it better? *The spotlight will kill you.*

The only way to keep the spotlight from killing me is to remember *I've already died.* In Christ, my life is not my own to hold on to or get credit for. I don't have to defend my name, display my talents, or demand attention.

If they don't know who you are, then you have been given the gift of obscurity. Let this not be offensive. Let this be a relief.

When I celebrate my smallness and receive the gift of obscurity, I am free. I have hope. I can give generously. I can be who I am rather than either who you think I am or who I *want* you to think I am. When I resist smallness it's because I'm afraid it means invisibility.

Jesus teaches me that *small* is a delightful place. To simply say what we hear our Father say, to move when he says move, speak when he says speak. It isn't about what we do but where we live. It isn't about what we have but who we are.

In turn, if you are a person who has some level of recognition, whether that be a prominent position in your community or some kind of national or even international stage, bear in mind that while your position might place you in the center, your soul isn't made to find life there. And when those spotlights burn brightly, imagine the light of Christ burning ever more brightly deep within you.

What It Really Means to Catch Your Big Break

In the creative circles where I often mingle, I'll hear people toss around phrases like "make it big" or "catch your big break," implying we're all waiting for some invisible access to success and everything that happens until then is just preparing us for the real thing. I'm sure most professions have similar language, always mindful of being one connection, conversation, or ladder rung away from a greater success. But waiting for your big break isn't Tuesday language.

What if your big break is really a breaking from big? What if your big break is you becoming acquainted with the suffering and brokenness of Jesus? We're called to live with Jesus and to embrace his downward way. We are not called to live by whatever means necessary as long as the ends look successful.

Jesus's ministry was marked by a rhythm of solitude, crowds, practical needs, hushing, leaving, hiding, and moving on. The book of Mark documents this so well, each chapter building on the last. And always throughout, after he performs a miracle, Jesus earnestly and repeatedly warns people not to tell what he did or who he is.

But of course they do, to the point where he can no longer travel through the big cities simply because the crowds are too large. So many places in Scripture document Jesus going away to be alone, almost hiding from the crowds. I've always thought it was the contemplative Christ who wanted to be with his Father; the praying Jesus.

But I wonder, and this may just be me, if he was doing something different. I wonder if he knew the human soul wasn't made for fame. And though he was God, he was also man and he knew how the people wanted to put a crown on his head and place him up on a stage on their terms.

"In the early morning, while it was still dark, Jesus got up, left the house, and went away to a secluded place, and was praying there" (Mark 1:35). The disciples came to find him, saying everyone was looking for him.

And he tells them, "Let us go somewhere else to the towns nearby, so that I may preach there also; for that is what I came for" (v. 38).

He doesn't shy away from his calling because it's somehow wrong to be famous. No, he continues to move, continues to preach, continues to heal. Fame is a result of all that for Jesus and he continues to move toward people, knowing he will get attention for it. But he doesn't continue for the purpose of recognition or attention. Fame might be a likely outcome but it makes a terrible goal. When it comes to rolling around in his own glory, Jesus never stops for that. He left all his glory behind with his Father in heaven.

Later, he tells them about how he will have to die. This is when Peter takes him aside and rebukes him and Jesus says,

"Get behind Me, Satan; for you are not setting your mind on God's interests, but man's" (Mark 8:33). At that point, Jesus gathers the crowd around him, using this moment to tell them something they may not at first understand.

"He summoned the crowd with His disciples, and said to them, 'If anyone wishes to come after Me, he must deny himself, and take up his cross and follow Me. For whoever wishes to save his life will lose it, but whoever loses his life for My sake and the gospel's will save it. For what does it profit a man to gain the whole world, and forfeit his soul? For what will a man give in exchange for his soul?" (Mark 8:34–37).

Before he became a wild success on *Everybody Loves Raymond*, Ray Romano lived in his parents' basement until he was almost thirty years old. He went from being an obscure stand-up comedian to a wealthy, successful, award-winning actor.

At the end of the show's nine-year run, he appears with the cast on the *The Oprah Winfrey* show and tells the story of when he first got cast. He and his family didn't know if his show would be a success, didn't know his would be a household name. As he packed to leave his home in New York for California, his brother tucked a note into his suitcase. Romano held on to the note for nine years and, after filming the final episode of the show, stood in front of the studio audience and read the words his brother wrote: "Good luck there with the show and remember what it says in the Bible, 'What does it profit a man if he gains the whole world but loses his soul?'"[3]

When Jesus first said those words, he summoned the crowd to hear it. He wanted as many as possible to know that gaining the world is nothing if you lose your soul in the process. In an interestingly ironic moment, when Ray Romano read those words on Oprah's stage, the audience clapped with great energy and appreciation. Somehow we all know those words are true, even if the person reading them is sitting on a stage on television. It resonates deeply within all of us, the importance of protecting our souls against the world, even as we reward those who seem to have everything with applause, money, attention, and acceptance. We know it isn't enough.

Six days later, Jesus took three disciples—Peter, James, and John—up to a high mountain and transfigured before them. Elijah and Moses showed up too. And Peter was so thrilled to be a part of this moment, so terrified and overwhelmed at the enormity of it, that he asked if they could build three tabernacles right there on the mountain, one each for Elijah, Moses, and Jesus. If he'd had an iPhone I'm sure he would have documented the whole thing for the internet.

Peter saw glory with his own eyes and instinct told him to worship, to build a tabernacle to house the glory. A voice from heaven spoke, saying, "This is My beloved Son, listen to Him!" (Mark 9:7). Suddenly, Peter, James, John, and Jesus were alone, like they'd been walking in a dream. Everything was back to normal. As they walked down that mountain, Jesus gave them orders not to tell anyone what they saw, and kept moving them on to the next city.

All the glory he left in heaven and he simply refused to accept any while on earth. It's like he was chasing small instead of big. And the small moments on Jesus's path were lined up like stones crossing over a river of glory. The people wanted to watch him jump in and claim it all, but he kept stepping on stones. After healings and miracles, he kept saying *hush*.

He knew what the disciples couldn't yet see. As he chased small on earth, he was really building the kingdom of heaven.

Stairwells & Stages

The last church where John served as a youth pastor is one of the biggest churches in our city. It's the same church where we were married fourteen years ago, but since then they've expanded to accommodate their growth. I lost my way the first time I tried to navigate the new building, going up and down the same stairwells, trying to figure out which floor I was on.

The first thing I noticed about those stairwells was they didn't have controlled air. So several flights up I started to feel the heat. It wasn't a place I wanted to linger.

It didn't take long for me to figure my way around the new building and climbing certain stairwells became a regular part of our Sunday morning routine. We would see friends going up as we walked down, stop to chat as people passed by.

But the stairwell itself was never a real destination. The purpose of the stairwell was to pass through, to get from one place to the other. The stairwell was a necessary pathway to the sanctuary. Never once did I consider how the stairwell could become a sanctuary itself. The youth group changed all that.

One Sunday night early in John's first year as the youth pastor, the students leading worship decided that, instead of keeping everyone in the youth group room like usual, they wanted to take us into one of the stairwells and sing together there. Evidently this was a regular thing and soon we learned why.

We piled in on the steps, squeezing beneath the platform overhang, crowding together on the floor, standing shoulder to shoulder against the cinder-block walls. One of the students led the group, and with the first note the voices of over a hundred high school students seemed to transform into a chorus of a thousand angels as each voice echoed ten times its normal amount.

We sat piled close in dim lighting, outside of our normal youth group room, singing several verses of favorite songs. There was a sense of community in the stairwell, a sense of simple wonder in discovering something so profoundly beautiful in someplace so dreadfully ordinary.

Part of why I think those stairwell songs remain so clear in my own memory is that I became less aware of myself in the stairwell as it was hard to tell whose voice belonged to whom. The collective sound was more beautiful than any one voice alone. Singing in the stairwell made it easy to see how ordinary places can become sanctuaries.

When we went back to the youth group room, I had to acknowledge a sense of disappointment as we assumed our usual posture—everyone sitting in darkness, no longer facing one another but angled toward the lit-up stage. And while I don't see a thing wrong with having a stage, I do recognize within myself the natural tendency I have, maybe one we all have, to assume important things happen on the stage and the stairwells are just a way to get there, one ordinary step at a time.

Tuesday is the stairwell of the week, the ordinary small day we have to move through to get to the weekend or to the seemingly more important tasks we have on our calendar. But what if we genuinely began to acknowledge the importance of both?

Don't elevate one at the expense of the other or de-elevate one to the exception of the other. I learn a lot about the state of my soul when I pay attention to the stages and the stairwells in my own life.

The stairwell can be a sacred place of worship or a secret place of fear. I can either move there on purpose or hide there from my purpose.

The stage can also be a sacred place of worship or a secret place of fear, a place I either move to on purpose or hide there from my purpose.

It wasn't impossible to experience wonder and community in the youth room, but the stairwell made it easy. Sometimes in life I forget about the beauty and connection that can happen in the stairwell and, instead, all my attention is focused on the stage. And while important things *do* happen on stages, while influence *does* come from spotlights, I never want to forget important things happen in stairwells too.

Christ spent his life on the stage of earth but he lived his moments in the stairwells of small towns. Christ ascended to the stage of heaven but he lives his moments now within the stairwell of the human heart. Never forsake the stairwell for the stage.

Since John served his last day as a youth pastor working at the church, we have loved much about this open time when he has not had a traditional job with traditional working hours. We are thankful for the space to do what I know many would benefit from but aren't able—financially or otherwise—to practice.

But we have also struggled on days. He literally went from that very youth room stage to no stage at all. Nobody wants their work to be underappreciated, undersold, or underwhelming. Ladders are for climbing and careers are for building. It doesn't make a lot of sense to leave something successful, thriving, and growing and step into nothing. But that's what John has done.

Rather than looking for a job out there, we are praying and watching as a job forms within him, within us. It doesn't have a lot of lines or definitions yet, but it has heart, motivation, and some small amount of clarity. Because, you see, I married a pastor.

The fact that he is not on a payroll at a church does not mean he isn't a pastor; it just means his pastoring looks different right now. It doesn't change his desire, his gifting, or his calling. In the past, he's pastored teenagers. In the future, he'll pastor others. Right now, he pastors our family. Christ is forming John's confidence around an identity outside of his job description and that can be hard at times. The days of the stage may not be behind him forever, but they are in the past for now. In the meantime, we are learning the beauty of ministering in the stairwells, of finding the benches meant for us, and of forming intimate connections with a few rather than casual connections with many.

In my own work, I sense a grief that accompanies small, a disappointment that highlights my own pride, stubbornness, and desire for credit and attention. But I also sense an invitation, one that brings a desire to commune with Christ and with others in a way that the big I think I want may not allow. Daily I'm given the opportunity to recognize the gift of obscurity, trusting that Christ is doing invisible kingdom work in the stairwells of everyday life.

A Prayer for the Stairwell Singers

May we stretch out in the fullness of small and move downward with gladness rather than upward in fear. May we let go of the constructed life and embrace a connected life, even if it leads to less. May we be marked more by our small moments than by our fast movements. May our small moments do more lasting good than our fast movements do harm. Be gracious to remind us that our souls aren't made for fame. May we receive the gift of obscurity with joy, gratitude, and a light heart.

Our Tuesday Work

Questions for Bench Dwellers

1. What is the evidence in your own life that tells you when hurry has won the battle in your soul?

2. In what areas is it most difficult for you to release outcomes?

3. Do you recognize your eight-foot assignment? What is your assignment today?

4. What is the truest thing about you?

5. In what ways do you fear your personality gets in the way of your desired success?

6. What are some stairwells and stages in your own life right now?

7. In what ways have these stairwells and stages informed your life, your calling, and your deepest desires?

Part 3

Finding Our TUESDAY People

More connecting. Less competing.

I'm beginning to see how the secret ways and deepest mysteries
of God and his kingdom are often revealed off the beaten path
of organized religion and frequently missed by the too-smart.
Sometimes it's not the professor or preacher leading you to
divine truth but the commonplace people God sticks right in
front of your face.

—Jim Palmer, *Divine Nobodies*

In this section, you are invited to:

- find a safe place to feel insecure
- replace the compulsion toward competition with the gift
  of connection
- move downward with gladness
- wear the world like a loose garment

COMMUNITY & COMPETITION

Finding Safe Places to Feel Insecure

With people, you can connect or compare but you can't do both.

—Shauna Niequist

Last spring was a difficult one for me. I was walking through a fog of loneliness and questioning and realized, after a period of time, that the fog might not be a temporary cloud but a new way of living.

In my loneliness, though I knew a lot of people and had many acquaintances, I doubted if any of them truly knew me. It was during this time that I realized I had two choices. I could either continue as I was, waiting for people to show up and surround me, or I could decide to move toward people myself. Would I rather people just come to me? Yes. Would I rather be pursued than pursue? Yes. But more than these, I would mostly just rather not feel so lonely.

Sometimes when I think I'm waiting on God I wonder if he's actually waiting on me. I looked at the areas of my life where I felt like I needed some company and I came up with three: my soul, my family, and my work.

Connection for My Soul

I feel like I need to talk with someone about all this foggy loneliness, but I'm not sure where to turn. After all, I haven't survived a tragedy, I'm not facing a life-threatening illness, and neither is anyone in my family right now. I have a lovely life with everything I need and most of what I want. But this deep loneliness is creeping into every small moment and I don't know what to do about it.

I've been to counseling before and that has been helpful at different times in my life. But this particular need doesn't feel like a counseling type of need. I have read a lot about spiritual direction, even took a course on it—more experiential than training.[1] The evangelical environment I grew up in, the one I'm in now, doesn't have a regular practice for spiritual direction, so I don't have a lot of people who can advise me on finding someone to meet with.

I don't trust anyone young, famous, or on the internet for this. I don't want to meet with anyone who knows who I am because of John's years as a pastor, because of the books I've written, or because of mutual friends. I don't want to risk meeting someone who might be easily impressed by me. Is that arrogant? Probably. But that's how I feel about things. I need to find someone I can't trick, fool, or manipulate. I long to feel small in the presence of someone else.

Upon the recommendation of a friend, I end up contacting Marion, an older woman living only a few miles from my house. In the email, I tell her I'm not exactly sure what I'm looking for, but I would like to meet with someone to help me sort that out. She explains spiritual direction is simply an ongoing process of opening to God's presence in your life with someone who holds a prayerful space for you to do that. Considering that one sentence description alone brought tears to my eyes, I figured this was something I needed to do.

My decision to meet with Marion is one I haven't regretted for a second. Over time, it's becoming a more necessary rhythm in my life, one I need and look forward to.

It's been six months since our initial meeting on the first day of Lent and we've had several in between. We met again this morning, a crisp, dark blue sky overhead. As we now approach Advent, I tell her this is my favorite season.

Fall is always a full time of year: the twins have their final volleyball games, many weekends I travel, first quarter report cards come home, school projects are in full swing, and end of the year deadlines start creeping up. I shared with Marion how I don't want to miss this season. I don't want to be moving through and then realize it's mid-January and I missed out on this part of my life.

Yesterday after church I made soup. I put on music, chopped carrots and celery, boiled chicken, and minced garlic. I warmed bread, added heavy dollops of butter on top, opened windows so I could hear the kids playing in the driveway while I worked in the kitchen, their laughter piercing the sound of the wind through the coloring leaves in the yard.

I did all of that, but all I told Marion was, "I made soup." And just when I realized how dumb that sounded, when I caught myself wanting to explain why making soup was a thing, she said something that surprised me.

"That's beautiful."

And I began to cry.

This simple act of making soup means I'm here, in this moment, engaging in something I love. Yesterday, making soup was a spiritual act of worship and Marion seemed to understand that. Better, she understood without me having to explain it.

In the power of the Spirit, Marion and I connected.

After I made the decision to move away from loneliness in my soul by meeting with Marion, I knew I also needed to open myself to connection in other areas as well.

Connection with Community

On the right-hand corner of my desk, right next to the books I'm currently reading, sits a small envelope holder where I keep notes friends have written. I didn't plan for it to become a prominent place, but every time I've received a note from someone in the actual mail, there it goes, right on my desk where I can see it every day, a reminder of my inability to do this on my own—this living and working and moving through life.

For the past several months I've been reading Thomas Merton's autobiography of faith, *The Seven Storey Mountain*. He writes in fascinating detail of the time he spent as a student at Columbia in New York, indulging in all of the things young students in the late 1930s could indulge in, resulting in "confusion and misery."

"Yet, strangely enough," Merton writes, "it was on this big factory of a campus that the Holy Ghost was waiting to show me the light, in His own light. And one of the chief means He used, and through which he operated, was human friendship."[2]

As I read those words, I thought of the role human friendship has played in my own life, how I have both craved and feared vulnerability, how I have sought connection but also denied my need for it.

When I was growing up, people said I made friends easily. Evidently a teacher once told my parents that I made friends quickly with other girls because I was always complimenting them. Having friends was important to me. But that was back when the word *friend* meant someone you're comfortable sitting with at lunch or someone who will walk with you to the bathroom so you don't have to go alone.

All that counts when you're in seventh grade. But now that I'm grown, friend means something more than that. Meeting people is easy for me and making good impressions is too. But now I want Tuesday people in my life, not people I work to impress. And when we consider the spiritual transformation of our lives, it often means being stretched beyond what comes natural and leaning hard into what is supernatural, those things that come from God. Learning to move toward community is often one of those unnatural-turned-supernatural things for me.

Nothing causes me to face my own humanity, frailty, and weakness more than when I am in communion with others. Nothing causes me to see myself as I really am, to admit I'm not as great as I think, or to face my perceived entitlements than when I am in the midst of other people. I am easy to live with in a room by myself. But I don't want to live in a room by myself. Not forever, anyway.

Friends have also been the gateway to my remembering and accepting the lovely parts of myself, the playful pieces of my personality I often leave behind. To know and be known is both compelling and repulsive to me. The way God moves on earth is through the hands and eyes and feet of people—both the ones I'm naturally drawn to and the ones who get on my nerves.

Since John left his job at our former church, we have been quietly attending a small church near downtown. The kids did well with the transition—but I am a woman who, as a girl, moved around churches and schools and states like it was my job (I only exaggerate a *little*) so I probably haven't given them much room to not do well. They haven't had to move houses or schools or anything. Just church.

I realize it isn't fair or thoughtful of me to filter their experience through my own. Just because I grew up with more extreme life transitions doesn't mean theirs isn't valid or difficult.

They haven't been thrilled with leaving what was familiar to them and we've made some space to talk about it. But this month, something is happening I didn't hope to expect. *They've started to like this new, small gathering of believers.* They've not wanted to miss a Sunday.

This past week, they sang one song during an evening service with the other children. They were eager to participate and seemed to have fun, but most of the kids are younger than they are. During group performances at our former church, they blended in with hundreds of other children. But here at our new church our daughter was the tallest one on stage and she didn't seem sure about how to handle that feeling. I don't think she'll want to do that again. Sometimes it hurts to grow up.

It's easy for me to tell her it's not a big deal that she's the tallest one and that her insecurities are unfounded. But flip it around to me and things don't feel so certain. As I watched her squirm in discomfort in this new surrounding, I saw myself in her. I recognize my own "I'm taller than everyone else" kinds of feelings, like when we started to attend a family community group as the newest members.

We meet each Sunday night, and because I don't know them well yet, I find myself questioning the words I say, the stories I choose to tell, and the silences I keep. I look around at this group we've joined who have known one another longer than they've known us and I recognize the feeling of sticking out, of being new, of being unknown. It hurts starting over with new people even though we chose it and even though it's right. But we continue to go because each week builds on the one before and slowly, over time, I am beginning to consider this small group to be among my Tuesday people.

A few months ago, our pastor announced at the end of the service how a prayer team had started to meet together every Thursday morning and if we had any requests, they would pray faithfully. When he said it, tears filled my eyes. Because I think it's important to pay attention to what makes me cry, I considered why that moment was emotional for me. My answer came swiftly: the idea of having a few huddle together who are willing to carry my requests to God on my behalf poked something awake in me, something I longed for.

After the benediction, I made my way to the back of the church and wrote out a simple request on a small white sheet, confessing my longing to find my people in this church, awkwardly asking for prayer in a few areas of my life. I folded it twice and tucked it into the thin slit on top of the box, all the time wondering if I got cancer or something happened to one of our kids, would I have people? Have I cultivated relationships over these years enough to warrant support from others in times of crisis? Or even just in times of regular?

A week later, I got a text message from Wendy, a new friend on the prayer team. These were her words: "You do have people—we love you and prayed for you today. Thanks for letting us come with you and keep us posted—we will be so happy to be praying with and for you!"

Her words were simple but also healing, because they reminded me that finding my Tuesday people doesn't have to involve a massive effort or an intricate, long-term plan. It also reminded me that while I'm often hesitant to reach out, my doing so is like giving a gift to others—the gift of trust, the gift of honesty, the gift of myself.

John and I have never been part of groups that vacation every summer together, take annual family camping trips, or go out as couples every other weekend. Sometimes I have these moments of relational panic when I see other families who seem so tightly knit that their kids are growing up together nearly like siblings. Are we missing out? Are we doing this friendship thing wrong?

We have dear friends and we love them, but it doesn't look like the movies. It looks like long stretches of months before we see them again for dinner. It looks like grabbing a coffee while the kids are in school. It looks like quick notes shared during difficult days over texting. It looks like slipping a prayer request in the wooden box in the back of the church.

I suppose we will have insecurities no matter where our feet take us. But we are continuing to walk to new places even though sometimes we find things we don't like. The benches we are invited to sit on with others may not always lead us to the security we long for. Sometimes they will simply provide us a safe place to feel insecure.

There are a few friends with whom I simply share everything, the moments when I am a saint and the ones when I'm a dirty-faced sinner. Sometimes when I let people see the falling-apartness within me, I second-guess my openness later, losing sleep or sending a frantic text of apology. But my true friends don't let me apologize for being human. They welcome me with all my junk and inconsistencies. I'm thankful for new friends, for the space to remember how the Spirit speaks to us, and for safe places to feel insecure.

Connection in My Work

Writing is a lonely profession. You sit in your little space with your computer and your thrice reheated cup of coffee and hope that your words are making sense or will make sense by the time someone reads them. It's lonely in the physical way that you literally write alone.

But it's lonely in other ways too; namely, the kind of loneliness that comes when you feel like no one around you understands the unique struggles of your job, the challenges you walk through, and the details of the daily work you do. I'm sure most jobs feel that way.

After writing a blog on the internet for over nine years, I have made many online connections with people who have become real-life friends. We email, we text, we have Facebook groups to offer encouragement and support as well as a space to ask questions. But I came to a place where I felt like I needed to hear these same words and encouragements from a friend sitting on my sofa rather than in my inbox. So I began to pray for a few women in my everyday life with whom I might meet, a small group to offer mutual encouragement and support, a Tuesday kind of group.

It sounds simple, maybe too simple. But you have to know this was a huge step of faith for me. I tend to go through cycles of loneliness, longing, anxiety, and then find just enough distraction to ease the loneliness a bit. I successfully numb the longing for connection and encouragement and don't reach out. Then a few months later, it all starts up again.

But as I've been waking up to my desire for connection, I didn't want to ignore the loneliness this time. I prayed to find a few women who live nearby, who do work similar to my work, whom I could trust and who I thought might trust me. After a few days, only one name came to mind. I texted her:

> Hi Amy—So I've been thinking for a while how I often feel lonely and discouraged in my work and I've decided to get intentional about it. I'm thinking about gathering a handful of local artists for mutual encouragement in our life and work—maybe to gather monthly? As I've thought of people to invite you come to mind. Is this even something you might be interested in?

She wrote back almost immediately. Her first words: "Lonely and discouraged would be an understatement. I would love this." We started brainstorming other women who might benefit from this and we both came up with Lara, another writer who lives locally. I texted her and her complete response was: "Yes. The end."

I make connection too hard sometimes. I have this idea that I need to find twenty people who understand me, and I need to find them now! But then I realize one or two really are enough. And so my longing for connection in my work led to our little group of three we casually call The Artists Circle, women journeying together every other month-ish. We meet at one of our houses or at a coffee shop or restaurant and ask three questions suggested by Todd Henry, who wrote *The Accidental Creative*:

What are you working on?

What is inspiring you?

Where do you need prodding?[3]

We also talk about family, fears, schooling, ailments—anything, really. But the best part is we do it on purpose and we do it together.

Competition, the Enemy of Connection

I continue to meet with Marion because I think God uses her as a mirror for me, to help me see the parts of myself that are hard to face. We continue to go to our little church on Sunday mornings and our community group on Sunday nights because the relationships we're building there, though sometimes slow and shy, are important to cultivate. I continue to meet with Amy and Lara because they remind me I'm not alone in my work even when I may feel alone. They remind me to have courage, to keep going, because, as my friend Annie says, "No one is brave alone."[4]

All of these connections also help me to embrace my whole person. Sometimes it's easier for me to accept the sin than it is for me to embrace the righteousness. But I need people to live with me as I learn to accept and embrace both.

One of the hardest parts of moving toward new people is never being sure what they're thinking of me. While I'm certain that is a consequence of my people-pleasing tendencies, I'm not convinced that's the extent of it. It's an issue of safety and control, which is a subtle form of competition, the enemy of connection.

Competition doesn't always mean I'm trying to win in the ways you might think. If I'm feeling anxious in a relationship and I stop to consider why, it's often because I'm competing on some level—for the upper hand, for control of opinions, for attention, for in-the-know-ness. If I don't think I have those things, I may try to get them. I'll put on my participant's number and begin warming up for the long race of gaining approval. And you know what a race means—competition.

The thing about competition is there is no time to connect with your competitors. You don't face them; you try to beat them. You're happiest when your back is to them because that means you're winning. And while that might work out just right in a footrace, it doesn't bode well for our relationships. How can I relate to you if I'm not facing you?

If I'm competing with you, I can't connect with you.

After a particularly difficult week, I looked forward to gathering with a small group of friends. I was in a hard place and knew being with them might help. I needed to be with people more than I needed to be alone, which is saying a lot for an introvert.

We sat around in the living room, a few on sofas, a couple on the floor, and someone asked me a question about how things were going. I started to share a few things, testing the waters. I wanted to tell them everything but I wasn't yet convinced they wanted to know. So I shared the easiest parts, holding the intimacies closer to my chest. They allowed a few silences, a couple asked follow-up questions, and I started to gain courage that they really wanted to hear me and were willing to walk with me into the difficult place I'd been traveling alone.

I paused again for a moment as I spoke, internally processing some of what I wanted to share before I said it out loud, and it was in that precise moment that one person spoke up and said with all the good intentions in the world, "Can we just pray for you right now? I really just want to pray."

So we closed our eyes, and everyone said a few words of prayer for me, and when that was done they moved on to the next person and my time was up.

My heart sank. Here I was, getting ready to share the most honest part of my story and someone interrupted and offered to pray. Listen, I love prayer. I do. I love talking to God and bringing requests to him and carrying burdens on behalf of others. But in that moment, I needed to meet Jesus through the eye contact of my friends, not through the closed eyes of prayer.

I longed for my friends to allow prayer to be a comma in this moment, a way to invite God into a conversation already happening. Instead, this prayer was used as a period. New paragraph. End of story. It felt like he didn't know what to do with me so he used prayer as a way to cut me off. I'm sure he didn't intend for it to feel this way to me. And I'm even hesitant sharing this now.

The truth is, people need our with-ness. They don't need for us to impress them with how spiritual we are. They need to know they aren't alone. People need us to embrace a relational smallness, accepting we are not the star, the counselor, the convincer, or the fixer. Instead, we are a companion, willing to keep company with the soul of another. We need not compete, we need only to connect.

Connections aren't always smooth and sometimes we trip over the wires. We move toward others but then we get scared, have second thoughts, apologize for being human, long for different responses from them. People disappoint us and we disappoint them and are left to wonder if it's worth it.

What I'm learning as I invite others to sit on the bench with me and as I find the courage to sit on the bench with them, is that it is absolutely worth it. My desire for connection forces me to sometimes have to sift through disappointments in not connecting in the ways I wish. But those desires have also led me to some of the most beautiful relational gifts I've experienced: Marion, our little church home, The Artists Circle, even my kind friend with the awkward prayer. I'm thankful for my Tuesday people who offer me safe places to feel insecure, and I hope to be a Tuesday person for others as well.

A Prayer for the Hesitant Connectors

We confess our fear of community—how we both crave and dread it at the same time. We confess our tendency to lurch and limp through interactions with people. May we be sensitive to the ways our words land in the hearts of others. May we be quick to turn to you when the words of others land heavy in ours. Show us the people you ask us to love and give us the courage to be loved in return.

CHILDREN & GROWN-UPS

An Invitation to Move Downward
with Gladness

I would not choose to become a child again but I am
looking to children and searching in them for a simplicity and ordinariness that makes being an adult easier
to accept and miracles easier to see.

—Macrina Wiederkehr, *Seasons of Your Heart*

We load up the car and drive halfway to Charlotte,
straight to the crowded parking lot of a fast-food
restaurant. It's mid-July and that means it's time
for Grandy Camp, five days in the summer when Mom and
Dad take our three kids and my sister's three kids and fun is
had by all.

Years ago we decided exit 76 off I-85 was about the halfway point, and so this is where we meet my parents and trade sleeping bags and excited children for an empty car and several days together, just John and me.

Not used to this kind of spacious time once we get back home, we reacquaint ourselves with one another in the form of him napping on one end of the sofa while I read a book on the other. We leave our empty house for an early dinner at a little Greek restaurant nearby and marvel at the space and the quiet that has now descended upon us.

After dinner we go shopping and browse through the organic foods grocery store, a place we rarely shop, and buy not one necessary thing—not one egg or gallon of milk. Instead, we leave with individual slices of over-priced dessert and a bottle of wine. His mom is out of town so we head straight to her house to eat our fancy cake and watch *Tiny House Nation* on her cable television.

When the kids aren't around, we kind of turn into them.

It's good for the parents to have some time away from the kids for lots of reasons, not the least of which being so we can remember how to be kids ourselves. I think of the words of Wess Stafford: "So far as we see in reading the Gospels, Jesus never admonished children to become more grownup. He did, however, exhort grownups to become more like children."[1]

He's always inviting us grown-up people downward with gladness, always pulling us closer to him, always welcoming us to the small places we sometimes forget to go when we are busy being the grown-ups. Since Jesus tells grown-ups to become like little children, it seems important to study what little children are like. Perhaps we'll be better at finding our Tuesday people when we know what we're looking for.

Little Children Follow the Agendas of Others

The day began hurried. I woke up with my mind already filled with things I needed to finish today, some household tasks, a few meetings, lunch at school with Luke, some deadlines I needed to meet. When I begin to write a list before the coffee is finished brewing, it's a sure sign that my body is trying to outrun my soul.

As parents, we want so badly for things to turn out well, for the kids to get into a good school, make right choices, be safe and cared for. But this desire sometimes ends up polluting all the Tuesday moments, and we accidentally find ourselves building cities all over the laundry and the leftovers.

I had a meeting first thing after dropping the kids off at school and I took a few minutes in prayer beforehand, approaching it more like a flu shot than a breath. I know this is good for me and I know it's necessary but it feels terribly inefficient.

But the Lord, he is gracious with me. With my eyes closed, Matthew 18:3 comes to mind, "Unless you are converted and become like children, you will not enter the kingdom of heaven." Immediately I envision Luke's preschool classroom, the one where we took him many years ago. I decide to stay with this picture in my mind for a moment during prayer, just to see where it leads me. I am praying, after all, so perhaps I should pay attention to what comes to mind.

God meets me sometimes in my imagination, stands at the doorway of all of my memories and invites me to walk with him there. He knows all the places I've been, all the scenes I've seen—both the ones I remember and the ones I don't—and he knows how to bring to mind those moments in time that I need to walk into when I'm ready and not a moment sooner.

In this moment during prayer, I stand in the doorway of the preschool classroom and walk inside, taking notice of all the tiny chairs and tables lined up, craft paper presented neatly at each place setting, names written in clear print on lined name cards.

I become aware that I'm not standing there as a parent or as the teacher preparing the class. Instead, I am the child, walking in to a classroom someone else has decorated to face a day someone else has planned. I am entering into their agenda and my soul is happy to be there. I pull out a chair and take my place at the table where I am not in charge but, still, I belong.

Unless you become like children, you will not enter the kingdom of heaven. This day belongs to the Lord. And he has set out craft paper and Play-Doh. This is the day the Lord has made for me to rejoice and be glad in. This is not the day Emily has made to toil and strive and earn.

Today, the banquet table is laid out for me in my soul. And it looks like meetings, deadlines, and a few household chores on the outside, but on the inside I know that my Father is very fond of me, that he has plans I know nothing about, and this is the day he has made. He invites me to come and sit at his table and pull up a chair made for small legs. He invites me to surrender myself to his agenda and trust that he intends good things.

Little Children Can Trust and Question at the Same Time

At the beginning of Luke 1, the narratives of Zacharias (or Zechariah in some translations) and Mary are interestingly similar. They are both visited by the angel Gabriel, both told not to be afraid, both told they will have a child. They both respond to the angel with emotion, they both ask the angel a question, but one ends up mute while the other skips away in praise.

Why? I read the passage again.

Zacharias was a priest who walked righteously in the sight of God. He was married to Elizabeth, but they had no children together because she was barren. It isn't too far-fetched to imagine there were people who believed them to be hiding some kind of secret sin, as barrenness was seen at the time to be evidence of disfavor before the Lord. In fact, at that time in history, husbands often left the marriage if their wives were unable to conceive as it was considered acceptable grounds for divorce. But Zacharias remained faithful. He stayed, he prayed, and he waited.

We meet Zacharias on one of the most important days of his life as a priest, the day he was chosen by lot from nearly a thousand priests to be the one to enter into the Holy Place. This is where he saw the angel Gabriel and immediately, the Bible says, Zacharias was "troubled" and "fear gripped him" (Luke 1:12).

But Gabriel reassures Zacharias, telling him not to be afraid. He says his prayers have been heard and his wife, Elizabeth, will have a son, and he is to give him the name John. And then Gabriel casts a beautiful, hopeful vision for their life, that there will be joy and gladness for not only their family but many people to come.

When the angel is finished, Zacharias responds by saying, "How will I know this for certain? For I am an old man and my wife is advanced in years" (v. 18).

There must have been something about the way Zacharias looked at the angel, must have been some tone of voice, some skepticism in his heart when he asked that question. Gabriel knows Zacharias doesn't believe, and as a result, Zacharias would be silenced and unable to speak until the day Elizabeth gave birth.

Zacharias was a good man, but he was also a *grown* man. A grown man knows when he's too old to get his wife pregnant. A grown man doesn't allow himself to get caught up in childish fantasies, fairy tales, and dreaming. A grown man knows when it's too late.

Perhaps he was too mature and filled with knowledge to receive a simple message from an angel who said he came straight from the presence of God. Zacharias was serious about God. Maybe that was his problem.

And then there is Mary—young, innocent, chosen.

When Gabriel came to her months after he appeared to Zacharias, he approached her in a similarly unexpected way. He called her "favored one" (v. 28) and told her the Lord was with her. I love the two things Gabriel did right away: affirmed her identity and reminded her she wasn't alone.

Presence is what we all need to feel secure. Presence was what Cain longed for when he left the Garden and built his own city. It's what babies long for when they cry in the night and what I long for when I feel lonely, afraid, or misunderstood. We were made for presence, and right away, Gabriel comforts both Mary and Zacharias with a promise of God's presence: *the Lord is with you* and *I am Gabriel, who stands in the presence of God.*

Similar to Zacharias, Mary didn't understand. And like he did with Zacharias, Gabriel casts a hopeful vision for Mary, telling her she would bear a son, and continues to explain what that will mean not only for her but for the whole world.

Like Zacharias, Mary asked the angel a question, "How can this be, since I am a virgin?" (v. 34).

Misunderstanding, a hopeful vision, a question asked. So far these two stories bear a striking resemblance.

Except the angel's answer to Mary is different from the one given to Zacharias. He comforts her with a promise of the Holy Spirit, reassures her that her baby will be called the Son of God, and even shares the news of her relative Elizabeth's pregnancy.

Both Zacharias and Mary ask a question, but only Zacharias must suffer a consequence. The angel answers Mary's question with a promise of with-ness, a vision for the future, and a person to relate to in the midst of her shock. He assures her the impossible would be made possible.

There must have been something about the way she looked at the angel, must have been some tone of voice, must have been some softness in her heart.

Zacharias asks a question and he is made silent in the presence of the people.

Mary asks a question and she is praised in the presence of God.

Zacharias was skeptical. Mary was open.

Zacharias doubted. Mary believed.

She must have asked a question like a child rather than like a grown-up. Her question was one of curiosity and wonder rather than doubt. We don't know exactly how old Zacharias was, but he was at least over forty at the time of the angel's visit and most believe he was older than that. Mary was believed to be between thirteen and sixteen.

Maybe his inability to speak was actually a deep act of love from God. He asked how he could know *for certain* and immediately he was unable to speak. This was his answer, a way for him to know "for certain" that the angel was telling the truth. It didn't take him nine months to believe, it probably took less than nine seconds. His inability to speak was proof, and I imagine he ran home to Elizabeth and their time together was deeply meaningful, sacred, and strong. I imagine he took her into his arms with the body of an old man but the renewed faith of one much younger.

Zacharias's name means "the Lord remembers," and in those nine months of silence, Zacharias remembered the faithfulness of the Lord. Perhaps he learned that *childlike* is not the same as *childish*. He got the proof he needed and it led him to belief, to praise, and to blessing.

I relate to Zacharias's need for proof but I admire Mary's childlike ability to believe without any proof at all.

Little Children Believe the Words They Hear

Small things have big influence. A little leaven can ruin the whole batch. A tiny rudder steers the whole ship. Faith the size of a mustard seed can move a whole mountain. An answer spoken softly turns away wrath. Even the most small, simple words can have long-lasting impact. No one teaches us this better than children.

An English teacher in school told me I was a great writer and I believed her back then. It was only a short comment written at the top of a paper. But it made a big impact.

I once heard a man tell a story about a camp counselor calling him a "trooper," and so the next several years he saw himself as a trooper. Years later, his teacher called him an artist, so he saw himself as an artist (and still does, by the way).

A school librarian encouraged author Beverly Cleary as a child, "reviving her love for reading once again. She encouraged her to look out for books that she could easily relate to. Not only did she encourage her to read but to write as well. It was she who gave her the hope that one day she could write for children."[2]

A small word said to a child by a trusted adult could shape the child's vocational choices, self-image, and future decisions. Likewise, the same small word said to a child, if meant to wound, could shape that child's choices in an equally negative way.

But Jesus tells us to become like children, and little children believe the words they hear. It isn't until we grow up and start to analyze things that we begin to doubt the truth we heard about ourselves when we were younger. We question, compare, and reconsider our identity.

If I simply and fully believed what Jesus says about me is true, then when I feel discouraged as I approach my work, I will remember *I am his workmanship, made to do good work for his glory* (see Eph. 2:10).

When I feel nervous over a conversation I dread, I will remember *I have not been given a spirit of fear, but one of power, love, and a sound mind* (see 2 Tim. 1:7 NKJV).

When I set my head on my pillow at night and shame creeps into my thoughts over my inability to measure up, keep up, or live up to expectations, I will set my mind instead on the fact that I have been set free from shame (see Rom. 6:18).

When I begin to feel the anxiety of the future rush into my present, like a child I can remember that my life is hidden with Christ in God and there is no safer place in all the world (see Col. 3:3).

Choosing to believe simple, true words about my identity is a childlike quality that often takes mature faith. What a difference this truth makes when I bring it into my Tuesday work and relationships.

Little Children Are Delightfully Messy

Recently I had a relational interaction that went not great. It went so not great, in fact, that I lost several nights' worth of sleep over it. I went over the conversation in my head at least a hundred times, imagining how I could have said what I meant more clearly, how I could have explained myself more thoroughly, and how I could have possibly avoided the outcome that was also—wait for it—not great.

As I prayed about the interaction several days later, it took a lot of effort to get present to Jesus in this place. Every time I became still, I remembered that hard conversation again and started to rehearse it. There's nothing more frustrating or discouraging than rehearsing something that's already happened. I kept getting caught up in the story of the interaction, unable to settle myself enough to listen to the truth. When I finally rested in silence, I tried to get down to the basic reason why this was so hard to let go. I came up with three.

1. I wasn't able to fully explain myself.
2. I knew the other person was disappointed in me.
3. I couldn't control what this person thought of me.

When I tried to come up with one word to describe how I felt about the whole interaction, the only word I could think of was *messy*. Working with people, loving people, getting along with people can get really messy. I don't like messy, I like clean and predictable. I like organized, controlled, and photographic. I do not like misunderstanding, conflict, or loose ends. I am a grown-up, you know.

Children are endlessly messy. But the beauty is that they are generally unaware of how messy they are. They aren't embarrassed over it, they don't try to hide it, and they certainly don't let their mess get in the way of moving toward others.

It's true—this uncomfortable interaction with this person could have gone better. I could have said things differently, approached it from a different perspective, and explained myself better. But I didn't, and it was messy. That is the simple truth. I'm thankful my Father doesn't expect me to get everything just right. I'm thankful he isn't only okay with my mess, but that he invites me to come away with him and to trust that he is with me even in the middle of it.

Childlike Souls, Grown-Up Obsessions

When you look at those Facebook questions I shared back in chapter 1, notice all the responses reveal something fascinating about our interior world—our souls are surprisingly young. We don't want to go first, be left out, be put down, ignored, or forgotten. We don't want to be wrong, embarrassed, or criticized. We can all relate to those fears, and so can every first grader I know.

You can't make a soul grow up. Our souls are young and always will be.

Jesus speaks to the interior soul, inviting the child within to come to him for validation, protection, and truth. We have to get it somewhere. No matter with whom we interact, we remain young in it. Oh, how young the souls of men and women. How delicate the skin around the heart. It isn't maturity that hardens us, it's pain.

I don't think the answer is to toughen up or grow up. Remember, Jesus never tells children to grow up. The answer to embarrassment, disregard, criticisms, and a thousand other flippant reminders throughout our day that we are not what we wish we were, the answer is not what we grown-ups tend to do—build, protect, figure a way to validate ourselves. The answer is not to convince others of our worth.

The answer is to accept the invitation of Jesus to be like little children and come to him because he knows on the inside we already are. He invites us not to stoop to become less than what we are, but to finally take on the truest shape of ourselves: a small and dependent child of God.

When we let ourselves become who we already are, we allow our souls to be a spacious foundation for the building of the kingdom of God. For that, we don't need a stage, a platform, a position, a title, recognition, reputation, or validation. It's simply Tuesday and we're simply children, sitting on benches, low to the ground.

A Prayer for the Childlike Souls

We confess our inability to move downward with gladness without your divine companionship. We know how much we despise the low places. But we are thankful for Jesus, who gave up everything to come be with us. May we release our obsession with order, agendas, proof, and planning. May we keep company with children, low to the ground. Help us to freely form the crayon circles and not be so particular about coloring within the lines. May we breathe in their slowness, keep pace with their rhythm, embrace their smallness, and let it be our own.

HONESTY & MATURITY

Learning to Relate
in the Power of the Spirit

God meets us where we are, not where we pretend to be.

—Dr. Larry Crabb

Here in North Carolina, winter comes long enough to make a snowman but doesn't stay long enough for you to turn into one. I'm thankful for the seasonal changes we experience here. I need the winter, the blanket of cold, the hush of nature. I need the reminder that new life comes when the old life dies.

Last week in church, we prayed a prayer during our time of corporate confession of sin. Here is the last part of that prayer: "Hollow out in us a space that you can fill with our transformed selves: peace, a whole heart, a forgiving spirit, holiness, and laughter. Fill us with yourself, we pray, for your sake, and the sake of the world."[1]

Guess what doesn't happen fast? The hollowing out.

Following this corporate confession, we sit for a time of silence to embrace the forgiveness that is already ours in Christ. I look forward to these few moments every week, moments of personal reflection in the midst of a room filled with people. And after the silence, we stand to move toward others for a few moments, a passing of the peace.

Every week without fail, I have to gather myself before meeting those around me. To turn from facing my sin to facing my neighbor is a difficult transition, and I always wish they would give us more time between silent confession and communing with others.

But that's the point, isn't it? Move toward others even as Christ moves within you. I am asked, invited really, to move toward others in my weakness. Though I've always believed this to be true, it is not easy or comfortable to practice. These few moments in church are a whisper compared to living it out in my life. But it's a rhythm I am beginning to embrace more now than ever before.

When Being Honest Means Being Mature

My first book, *Grace for the Good Girl*, was a book that nearly wrote itself. Not because it was easy, but because I had so much I wanted to cram into that book. I couldn't write fast enough.

But one chapter I worked on longer than all the rest. That chapter was called "With a Wink and a Smile: Hiding behind

Her Fake Fine." I wrestled with it, worried that it was coming across like we always have to tell everyone all the time how we feel about everything. And I don't think that's true.

Not only that, some gatherings simply aren't safe places for vulnerability. And sometimes the problem isn't vulnerability but that we don't know what to do when people are vulnerable. So we all sit around a room and "be vulnerable." Then what? What comes next?

Sometimes not sharing how we feel isn't an issue of hiding but one of maturity. Knowing we have died with Christ and inhabit the invisible kingdom of God means in Christ we *are* fine even when we don't feel fine. But that inner knowing often comes only after years of practicing faith. It's a layered, nuanced reality, and I wasn't sure I could find the words to communicate that tension.

In the end I wrote the chapter as best I could, leaving it as it was because I was convinced the women who needed to hear it outnumbered those who would misunderstand it. But over the years I have continued to struggle through this balance (for lack of a better word) of not hiding behind fake fines while also embracing my security in Christ, realizing sometimes it's okay to struggle and not share it because maybe I'm traveling a personal journey and don't always need to tell everyone about it. And that doesn't mean I'm being fake, it just means I'm honoring my own design, personality, and process.

I'm always on the lookout for authors and thinkers to shed light on those areas where I struggle to articulate something. Reading Heather King's *Shirt of Flame* brought me a few steps closer to understanding one side of this particular struggle.

In her book, she shared the example of enjoying your own birthday party, all the attention on you, and then a friend decides to announce her pregnancy right in the middle of it. "We take a bit of a backseat and rejoice for her with the rest of the guests. That's not dishonesty, that's maturity. That's refraining from making every little thing about us. That's caring about the spiritual well-being of another. That's wearing the world like a loose garment."[2]

Something within my soul clicked in this statement, wearing the world like a loose garment. A loose garment leaves room to breathe, holds lightly to expectation, doesn't show all the curves. A loose garment allows margin to move without restriction. A loose garment doesn't reveal every curve and secret. It leaves a little room for mystery.

A garment is loose when we are small within it, when we don't fill it out all the way. I imagine a small child pulling on his daddy's extra-large T-shirt, swimming around in all the extra fabric. There is room to move and also room to grow. The world need not meet my needs and sometimes it's good that the world not know what they are. Instead, I wear the world loosely, open-handed, light. I recognize some things are best kept between me and Jesus and I can trust him to carry my hurts, joys, and longings close to his heart.

This loose garment metaphor has taken deep root in my heart, especially since I recently cleaned out my closet, ridding my wardrobe of all those too-tight jeans I've been holding on to. Though I loved the idea of those jeans, I began to notice how irritable, negative, and touchy I became when I wore them, ever more eager for the day to end so I could peel them off and put on my big girl pants. When I'm around people who wear the world too tightly, their touchiness, judgments, and irritabilities wear off on me too.

I want to continue to learn how to wear the world like a loose garment as well as pay attention to the people around me who are doing the same. And together we'll wear our baggy shirts and keep company with Christ as we remember not to take ourselves too seriously.

When Being Mature Means Being Honest

Still, we can't discount those times when we are asked to move into the chaos of community without any guarantees of safety or discretion. There are times when we are to admit something has wounded or bothered us even when we feel silly for letting it.

For days I've been trying to think of a time when something bothered me and I was honest about it. It's been close to impossible. Not because things don't bother me, but because I tend to err on the side of silence when they do. As much as I wish I could claim loose-garment status in every situation, I can't, and I don't even think that's the goal.

After thinking through my relational interactions over the past several months, one particularly stressful gathering comes to mind. I had planned an event for several months and finally the day came to host it. Things went mostly as planned and once the event was over I was relieved to drive home with a friend, thankful for her company with the full expectation we would spend most of the hour drive reflecting on the event, our impressions of it, and a general feeling of relief and celebration that it was over.

Instead, the conversation took a turn I didn't expect, one where she ended up sharing some of her own struggles and thoughts she needed to work through. So instead of being encouraged on the ride home, I found myself needing to actively listen and be the one doing the encouraging.

I felt a tension inside me, pulling in two directions. On the one hand, I was glad to listen and to encourage. On the other hand, I desperately wanted to be listened to and encouraged myself. And I felt selfish and foolish for feeling that way. I didn't want to make every little thing about me, wanted to "wear the world like a loose garment" in this situation.

But the next morning when it was still on my mind, I knew I needed to talk with her about it even though I was embarrassed. The truth is, it wasn't wrong of her to share how she was feeling on the way home. But I felt like I needed to tell her how I was feeling too. I knew the risk of letting her see what seemed to me like a childish hurt was a better choice than the risk of allowing this to fester within me.

When I finally talked honestly with her about my feelings, she was gracious and kind, even more than I would have imagined. She didn't laugh at me or say I was being ridiculous or get mad at me for bringing it up. She listened. She related. She sat with me on the bench and offered me her company. I was so glad to have her there.

Looking back, I know that it would have been easier not to tell her because it seemed so ridiculous and small. It would have been easier to pretend I wasn't bothered and to move ahead with my low-maintenance reputation in tact. But the most important thing isn't that I seem breezy and laid-back in every interaction; rather it's that I am honestly connecting with the people I love.

It's good for me to feel the pain of humility in the presence of others and to remember my own emotions about things may not tell the whole truth about the situation, but perhaps those emotions reveal some truth about me. The decision concerning when to speak up and let others in or when to stay silent requires discernment in the presence of God.

In her book *Mudhouse Sabbath*, Lauren Winner reflects on how it feels to risk letting other people in. "Asking people into my life is not so different from asking them into my apartment. Like my apartment, my interior life is never going to be wholly respectable, cleaned up, and gleaming. But that is where I live. In the certitude of God, I ought to be able to risk issuing the occasional invitation."[3]

In the midst of relationships that can be filled with both the grand moments of massive miscommunications as well as the small moments of awkwardness or absentminded disregard, I'm learning to "ask people into my apartment" as well as "wear the world like a loose garment."

The best way to learn what it means to be both honest and mature in relationships is to bring my small moments into the presence of Christ and trust that he will lead my next steps in a way that will move the relationship forward.

Footnotes and Headlines

Here are some questions that help me navigate honesty and maturity in my relationships:

Am I being honest for the sake of the relationship or at the expense of it?

Am I moving toward another in the new energy of the Spirit or the old energy of my flesh?

Am I trying to matter?

My friend Kendra makes it easy to be honest because when I risk telling her she hurt my feelings, I know she will listen to me, and not only listen but actually hear me and see me. She is quick to apologize, quick to put herself in my shoes, slow to anger and be defensive. This is a groove in our friendship I am deeply thankful for, one that has been carved out over many years, conversations, texts, interactions, and even conflict. She is a safe place for me to be insecure.

Sometimes I stay quiet out of fear and hiding. Other times it's from wisdom and maturity. On the outside, the difference might be hard to tell, but on the inside it's not a small, indiscriminate thing. On the soul level, it's a top story, whereas on the body level, it may be just a footnote.

And that's part of what it means to live fully on the simple Tuesdays. It means realizing the most real and true place where we walk around isn't on the worn-out carpet of our living room, but upon the delicate ground of the human soul.

What our eyes see is a tired routine, but our souls are engaged in a new regime.

What if we began to approach our interactions as ones that exist in the invisible kingdom?

Sometimes I'll have a footnote interaction with someone, something that wasn't that big of a deal but somewhere deep in the soul level, it lands sharp. It isn't noticeable on the outside, but on the inside, it starts to cut. I had one such footnote interaction with someone yesterday that grew into a top story of my soul.

This morning, I woke up bothered, some irritation lingering just outside my awareness. As I made coffee, I couldn't quite place where it was coming from so I began to re-trace my steps over the last twenty-four hours or so.

What moment disrupted the good day I was having? It doesn't always work, this peace-of-mind rescue mission. This time, though, a small conversation came to mind that I realized was the source of this morning's discontent.

Yesterday we celebrated a birthday with a group of friends, gathered around the table, ate meat, had cake, and watched the birthday girl open presents. Because of all the children and activity surrounding birthdays, the kinds of conversations around the table are more half-conversations, and I was engaged in one such half-conversation toward the end of the meal. A friend asked me how I was doing and what my schedule was like these days. I shared some minor details with her, how these weeks are my most full weeks of the year. I would say "busy," but I've grown to dislike that word.

So I shared with her about the surface-y state of things and her brow furrowed and I could tell she was concerned even though I wasn't expressing any concern myself. What happened next was innocent enough. She kindly said, "I hope you're able to get a break soon." That's all she said and I know she meant it.

I casually agreed, and then we were distracted by birthday singing and the rest of the night's festivities. From then on, I was bothered but didn't exactly realize it, even though on the way home I was having conversations with her in my head. *Well, this is my job,* I thought to myself. *Just because my job requires travel does not automatically mean my soul is in a state of disrepair or that I'm not getting the rest I need.*

I was defensive and bothered. I began to analyze the expression on her face, reading into every nuance, attaching meaning that wasn't there. I decided her words didn't just communicate concern. I read them as judgment. With her mouth she said, "I hope you're able to get a break soon," but I imagined she actually meant, *You have too much going on and you are neglecting your children and your husband and your house and your dog and you're basically a terrible person.*

As I pour my coffee, my heart begins to beat faster in my chest. The anger whooshes through me all over again. Statements of defense and protection race through my mind. I grab on to a few to save for later. And then, because I'm in the middle of writing this chapter, two words come to mind: *honesty* and *maturity*.

In this moment, when I am angry and offended, what is the honest and mature thing to do? Call her up and tell her how I felt when she said those words? Maybe. Probably not. Especially since deep down I know I'm overreacting.

This morning, I'm sensing a subtle invitation, clandestine in its presentation especially in the midst of all my loud and varied emotions. The invitation is not a plan for me to confront her. Instead, it's a personal invitation to sit on a bench in the quiet for a while and be honest, not with her, but with myself.

The truth is, it wasn't her words that hurt me, it was my own ideas about what her words meant. It wasn't her thoughts that condemned me or her supposed judgment that caused my anger. It was my own, stemming from dormant fear and residual shame. Her words poked too close to something that already exists within me, a fear that I'm moving too fast and doing too much. Whether that's true isn't the current issue.

If I were to go to her and tell her all my thoughts and feelings about that interaction, maybe our relationship would grow, but more likely I would feel compelled to blame her and defend myself. This would keep me in the struggle for power and attention and validation, the earthly way of the world.

Instead, this quiet Tuesday invitation of the Spirit is whispering to me this morning, *Emily, the delicate grass of the kingdom is being formed in you. Don't trample all over the seeds. Instead, sit down and see what I am growing.*

I recognize a rebellious streak in me when it comes to this. Most of the time I'd rather stomp on the sprouts of growth than stand on tiptoe to see the faint outline of hope. I don't want to live in an invisible kingdom. I want to be in charge of this one, the one I can see and other people can see, the one where I can try to convince everyone to understand me. The one where I have control.

Seeing the Kingdom One Inch above the Ground

Before I can be mature, I have to be honest—not necessarily with others but with myself. Even writing this, it all seems silly. How can you write so much about a dumb interaction when people in the world are starving and dying and there are real problems at hand? That's a legitimate question, isn't it? Here's why—the dumb interactions are where we live during the Tuesdays of our lives. Until we begin to be honest about how these small interactions are shaping and forming us into either the ways of our earthly kingdoms or the ways of the eternal kingdom, we won't know how to move into the brokenness of the world simply because we haven't let Christ move into the brokenness of our own souls.

That doesn't mean we are to wait until we have all our junk figured out before we move. But it does mean there is a place, an important place, to discover how our small interactions with the people of God affect the kingdom of God. Until I'm willing to be honest with myself about the shape of my own soul, I will not be able to mature in my walk with the Spirit.

John Ortberg tells a story about an antagonistic student in one of Dallas Willard's classes. The student, obviously trying to get a reaction out of Dallas, made an argumentative point. Others in the class waited for Dallas to set that student straight. *Let 'em have it, Dallas!* I would have been thinking that too.

Instead, Dallas said he thought that was a good place to end the class, choosing not to respond to the antagonistic student at all. When asked later why he didn't let that student have it, Dallas's simple response was, "I'm practicing the discipline of not having the last word."[4]

These small moments, these seemingly insignificant interactions with people each hold within them the mystery of Christ in you. The hope of glory shows himself in the smallest of ways, in the midst of the most mundane tasks and annoying conversations. No matter what, I always have the choice to honestly get present to Jesus, to turn to him in the middle and consider what he's up to in my soul as well as in the souls of others. The kingdom of God is being built with materials I can't hold but I can see if I know where to look.

A Prayer for the Loose-Garment Wearers

We confess our inability to discern the difference between honesty and self-defensiveness, maturity and martyrdom. May we invite you into our footnote interactions so they don't fester into headlines. May we hand over every moment into your care, trusting you to handle us tenderly. And in the handing over, may the world become to us like a loose garment. May we have the courage to know when to speak and when to stay silent, ever moving toward others even as you move within us. May Christ be our security when we care too much about the little things and our salvation when we care too little about the big ones. May we have the insight, discernment, and humility to know the difference.

Our Tuesday People

Questions for Bench Dwellers

1. What part has friendship played in your spiritual formation?

2. Where are your safe places to feel insecure?

3. Which is the hardest to let go: your agenda, your need for proof, your negative concept of yourself, or the need for a mess-free life?

4. What small words have made the biggest difference in your life?

5. In what ways have you experienced the tension of "wearing the world like a loose garment" and "inviting others into your apartment"?

6. Is it more difficult for you to be honest with others or with yourself?

Part 4

Accepting
Our TUESDAY Soul

More laughter. Less shame.

We stop, whether by choice or through circumstance, so that we can be alert and attentive and receptive to what God is doing in and for us, in and for others, on the way. We wait for our souls to catch up with our bodies.

—Eugene Peterson, *The Jesus Way*

In this section, you are invited to:

- create a safe space for your soul to come out
- hold on to hope even in the midst of disappointment
- find quiet relief for your tired soul
- learn to laugh again

PRAYER & QUESTIONS

Making Friends with the Fog

> There are very few places where the soul is truly safe,
> where the knowing, the questions, the longings of the
> soul are welcomed, received, and listened to rather than
> evaluated, judged, or beaten out of us.
>
> —Ruth Haley Barton

Clouds roll into Greensboro the morning I go to see
Marion for the first time. It is the first day of Lent,
a time for preparation, for turning, for repentance.
I didn't plan our appointment that way on purpose, but it is
just as well.

I have been lonely for a long time by now; lonely for myself,
for the person I know I am, for Christ—near me and in me.

Unlike many of my Gen-X peers, many of us creeping toward forty, I haven't lived through a notable loss and rediscovery of faith or a deep doubt spiraling into angst or frustration with God and/or the church.

I am not angry. I just feel alone. Perhaps this is more common than I know.

The newness of a writing career is beginning to wear off. After several years of writing books and speaking engagements, I am becoming more introverted and private, less comfortable among strangers, more suspicious of people, less inclined to move toward longtime friends. And while I am experiencing a deeper intimacy with John and the kids, God seems far away. I am less aware of his presence and his peace.

All these mores and lesses begin to terrify me.

The Importance of Fumbling through Silence

Today is our day to meet, and she welcomes me into her sunroom, shadowed by clouds but warm with her presence. She has never heard of me or of John. Good start.

She introduces our time with silence and invites me to close it by saying *amen*. She bows her head, closes her eyes, and I do the same. Ten seconds in, I'm immediately stressed out. Am I taking too long? Not long enough? How long do people usually wait? The truth is, I could sit in silence the entire hour. But that's probably not what people do. Or is it?

I know I need this intentional space for my soul. I value being quiet and still in the deepest part of who I am. But in these moments of silence, I'm not sure what to do with myself. This fast-moving world supports a language the soul doesn't speak and it takes courage to emerge in a land that isn't home.

Today it's time to practice creating a safe space for my soul to come out.

Parker Palmer says the soul "speaks its truth only under quiet, inviting, and trustworthy conditions. The soul is like a wild animal—tough, resilient, savvy, self-sufficient, and yet exceedingly shy. If we want to see a wild animal, the last thing we should do is to go crashing through the woods, shouting for the creature to come out. But if we are willing to walk quietly into the woods and sit silently for an hour or two at the base of a tree, the creature we are waiting for may well emerge."[1]

I'm not sure Marion was prepared for me to sit on her sun-room sofa for an hour or two waiting for my soul to come out. But in that moment, it felt like I might need that kind of time.

It's true that our souls are like wild animals. It is also true that our souls are like little children. If the soul senses judgment, criticism, or rejection, she won't feel safe.

The problem is that one of her harshest critics is me. As I enter into this thoughtful place, my soul is already too intimidated by expectations to come out. I catch myself trying to figure out the right way to breathe, to pray, to listen. I don't want to mess this up. The very reason I came to meet with Marion shows up, right here in the beginning. I need a place free of expectation, yet here I am putting all these expectations on myself. After several minutes roll by with me fumbling through silence, I finally say *amen*. It wasn't a perfect silence, but it was a start.

The rest of our time progresses more easily for me. She asks a few questions and I talk in a direction that makes sense. I tell her about how when my father-in-law died in 2011, the grief both swallowed John and woke him up. I told her about our decision to leave his job at our church, about what we're doing now that he isn't a pastor at a church anymore, about how that feels.

As I continue to talk, I realize I am telling her mostly about John's life, about circumstances in our life together, but I recognize my inability to speak to where I am right now and how God is moving within me in this moment. I feel weird about that and I tell her so, but she reassures me this is actually the point of spiritual direction—we are often able to recognize God's presence and movement in other people, but are rarely able to see how he is present and moving within us personally.

As I continue to speak about our former church, my tears and the depth of emotion that comes up when I tell her I miss it surprise me. I knew I missed it, but I didn't know how deep it went—the people, the job, and the respect that comes with being married to a pastor. Even more, I miss what that church represented for me: control, answers, and predictable faith.

I was so happy to leave behind the hard parts that I haven't taken the time to grieve the good ones. It feels important for me to recognize this. "Parts of your life have been turned upside down," she says, "and it sounds like you're in a bit of a fog."

Until she says it, I don't realize how badly I need to hear it. I haven't been comfortable to admit those things because all of this was our own choosing. And we aren't dying or in poverty or in need of basic necessities.

My friend and author Leeana Tankersley says often we fear if we admit we're struggling, it may mean we're not grateful. But the truth is, we can be struggling and grateful at the same time. I think I recognize in myself a hesitancy to admit my struggle for fear it will incriminate me, branding me as a woman who has a beautiful life but doesn't appreciate it.

Maybe I've discounted and pushed aside the transition be-cause I've wanted to rush ahead to the next good thing. Through tears, I tell Marion I am surprised by my own emotion. I share about my struggle between seeking depth personally with Christ and feeling the need to package that into something to offer others. She then asks me which person in the Bible I most closely relate to right now. I consider her question.

Recently I've been reading in Matthew 11. Not the lovely verses at the end we quote so much—*Come to me, all who are weary*. I've been reading the beginning, the part where a jailed John the Baptist questions Jesus, sending a message through his disciples: *Are you the Expected One, or shall we look for someone else?*

I immediately answer Marion, telling her how John the Bap-tist is the one I relate to the most lately, though I'm not com-pletely sure why. She advises me to spend some time with him.

The Importance of Finding Company for Our Soul

In the days following our time together, I become acquainted with him—John, before he took his first breath of earth-air, the one who leapt in Elizabeth's womb, consumed by the pres-ence of Christ at the sound of Mary's voice; John, a man who prepared the way and spoke the truth and lived wild; John, a man whose entire life pointed like a locust-colored arrow firmly in one Christ-centered direction.

His was the opening act, the introduction to the Messiah. He ate bugs and lived in the wilderness and did all of these things because he couldn't not do them. It was in him to speak out, to point, to warn, to call, to prepare the way of the Lord. He abstained from food, drink, even normal clothing. He was fiery and passionate and unique, but not for the sake of being different. He knew the call of God on his life and he lived like it was true.

Good to know, but this description of John isn't particularly relate-able to me right now.

But then I look at John's life after he baptized Jesus and something changes. Maybe for John it all felt a little anticlimactic, the whole voice-in-the-wilderness thing. His life, already characterized by the loneliness of a prophet, has become even lonelier after he was arrested for standing up against Herod. And I imagine, as he sits in jail, he has some time to look over his life and considers the painful truth: Jesus didn't look anything like John expected him to look.

While John lived a life of self-denial, Jesus seemed to live a life of indulgence. People called John mental but they called Jesus drunk and even a few times accused him of being mad, as if he had lost his mind. Not only that, Jesus lived for thirty years without doing any ministry at all. At least, nothing obvious. Perhaps nothing worth the wilderness.

Maybe John initially embraced his lonely beginning as a prophet because he knew the arrows pointed to the Messiah. When he saw how his own message was spreading far and wide, maybe he began to form an expectation for what was to come. John had a massive following of people, and he was only there to prepare the way! Imagine what would happen when Jesus finally came. Surely the Messiah would bring a big ending. But all Jesus seemed to be bringing for John was more smallness and loss. This man who had lived his entire life in the openness of nature was now confined to the darkness of a prison cell. He had been faithful to his calling, and this was the outcome of his faithfulness.

The things Jesus was doing and saying didn't match with the Jewish expectation of the Messiah. He was expected to free Israel from bondage, but she was still under Rome. He was expected to stop all suffering and disease, but people were still sick. Even though Jesus had performed miracles, he certainly hadn't healed everyone. Perhaps the biggest disappointment was that Jesus himself refused to let the people make him king. So not only was there no new visible kingdom on earth, Jesus wasn't even doing anything about the current pagan one.[2]

And so after some time in prison—many believe it to have been about a year—John the Baptist needs some confirmation. He asks his disciples who have come to see him to ask Jesus a question on his behalf: *Are you the Expected One, or shall we look for someone else?*

At dinner last night, Luke reads a riddle with the word *journey* in it. I ask him if he knows what the word means and he says no. One of the girls speaks up, ready with a definition. "It means to go on a journey." I challenge her to define the word without actually using it in the definition. She has a hard time coming up with a different answer.

Going to Jesus when you doubt Jesus seems kind of like using a word in its own definition. Why would you ask someone you doubt to confirm the thing you doubt? Shouldn't you go to a different source? If John didn't think Jesus was the One they had been waiting for, it doesn't seem to me he would go to Jesus to confirm it. But he does. Which seems to indicate that even though John believed intellectually that Jesus was the Messiah, he had little experiential evidence to work with. Though he knew the truth in his mind, his heart was downcast. His was a relational question, not a theological one. This seems important for my soul to understand.

When Marion asked me which person in the Bible I most closely related to these days, my mouth answered before my mind could decide. I was surprised by it, surprised to hear John the Baptist's name come out. But I was relieved to hear it, relieved to have a name to go with this loneliness, relieved to have someone to relate to in it.

Seeing in the Dark

The more I spend time with this passage, the less likely it seems to me that John is angry or suspicious. As I read it and sit with these words, it just seems like he is feeling tired, lonely, and small.

Who would choose this smallness, this forgotten place? Not me. I wouldn't choose it. But I experience it anyway. My questions haven't steered my faith toward anger or fist shaking. Instead, my faith is walking into a deep loneliness, fear, and smallness. Maybe that's why Jesus's response to John's question from the darkness feels especially important to me.

Here is a man who is questioning, not just his entire life's purpose, but God himself; a man who seems disappointed in the way things are turning out. How will Jesus handle the doubt, the fear, and the feeble voice from the darkness? What does God say when questioned? Will he reprimand John for his lack of faith?

None of this. Instead, he simply points to two places.

First, he points outward, telling John's friends to listen, look, and then tell John what they observe—blind people see, lame people walk, deaf people hear, sick people are made well. John would recognize these outcomes as ones prophesied by Isaiah (Isa. 35; 61). In other words, *evidence of me is everywhere.*

But then, just as John's friends are walking away to deliver the answer, Jesus turns to the crowd and begins to talk about John. "Truly I say to you, among those born of women there has not arisen anyone greater than John the Baptist" (Matt. 11:11).

Jesus praises John in the midst of what was perhaps the darkest, most discouraging time of John's life. Yes, he points outward at the evidence of his presence. But this isn't the part that reaches down into me and touches something true. The part that makes me cry is when Jesus shifts from pointing out there to pointing within to the heart of John himself.

In other words, *my works are evident in the world, but my life is evident within you.*

Immanuel, God with us. Perhaps this unconventional Messiah is establishing a kingdom after all.

He does this for John's benefit, I know. He loves John, wants him to know he is not forgotten, even in his smallness. And he's reminding John that his is a life of faith and trust, not experience and sight.

Maybe Jesus speaks these words out loud for me as well, knowing people are listening, knowing Matthew will write it down, knowing soon he will go away and send his own Spirit in his place, knowing one day he will make his home within his people and they will never be alone, knowing I am one of those people, knowing I need to hear these words too.

Does he speak this to me when I am in my own crisis? Does he remind me of the track record of his faithfulness in the world around me even when it feels dark and lonely and off-balance? Does he gesture intimately, kindly, fully back toward me and remind me that not only has he been faithful out there but also he is faithful within me? And he has made my heart his home?

Even if I can't feel him. Even when I question him. Even in the darkness. Even when I am unsure.

I don't know if John *really* wondered if Jesus was the one. Maybe he just wanted Jesus to know he was struggling. And Jesus responds to him in the best way. No reprimands. No scolding for the question. Just love.

To me, Jesus's response to John's question is a bench for John's soul. Though many expected the Messiah to sit on a throne, instead he offers a bench of understanding, of love, and of compassion. Jesus invites John to come sit, wait, and hope in his presence, always whispering, *I will not leave you alone.*

It helps to know what's happening in the rooms of our soul, to turn on the lights or, if we're not quite ready for that, to at least light a candle. What are the shapes here? What looks familiar? What feels odd, uncomfortable, and unwelcome? What am I holding on to that I no longer need? What am I looking for, longing for, needing more of?

What did I expect? Where have I been disappointed? What am I waiting for? Am I willing to wait a little longer?

John needed Jesus to know he was struggling in prison. I need Jesus to know this too.

The prison of confusion.
The prison of no answers.
The prison of waiting.

As soon as I name these prison cells, I begin to wonder if they aren't prison cells at all.

Maybe the answer isn't in trying so hard to find the light but in being willing to face the fog and remember Christ stands here too. To remember together with all the saints that he is sufficient in the light and in the darkness, in the pain and in the joy, in the morning as well as the night. Maybe the answer is to agree with John the Baptist that Jesus looks nothing like I think he should look, speaks nothing like I thought he would speak, allows things I don't think he should allow. I need to confess my fear in confessing that and face my longing for more. I need to remember Jesus is enough even when he doesn't feel like enough. I need to tell him so, to question him, and to be willing to receive his answers of love, of hope, and with-ness that sometimes don't feel like answers at all.

The loveliest part of John's question is that he goes to Jesus with it. When we talk to Jesus now, we call it praying. When Jesus's friends talked to him on earth, maybe they were praying too—the kind you do with your eyes open, the kind you do face-to-face, the kind called conversation. What else would it have been?

John feels alone and sends a prayer question with his friends to God: *Are you the Expected One, or shall we look for someone else?*

How might my questions change if I was willing to pray them? Maybe they won't change at all. I realize it's worth finding out. All of this—the questioning, the wondering, the traveling through the fog—it all reminds me good things can happen here. Not feel-good things, but true-good things.

In her book *Learning to Walk in the Dark*, Barbara Brown Taylor offers an important reminder for those of us facing the fog. "If we decide to keep going beyond the point where our eyes or minds are any help to us, we may finally arrive at the pinnacle of the spiritual journey towards God, which exists in complete and dazzling darkness."[3]

169

I admit I don't like where this is going. This fog is beginning to feel less like a season and more like a lifestyle. Still, I'm thankful that Jesus gives me space to fumble through the silence and I'm learning that he meets me here in ways I would never expect.

A Prayer for Those Sitting in the Fog

We confess our love of cloudless days, bright mornings, clearly marked pathways. We confess our discomfort in the fog but recognize a longing we discover there too. Even as we confess our desire for answers, may we learn to walk humbly with questions. Help us to find your company beside us as we crouch in the darkness and wait for the first light of dawn. Help us to know your presence in ways we may have otherwise overlooked if not for our inability to see.

DESIRE &
DISAPPOINTMENT

Why Clarity Is Overrated

> Desire and desperation are the twin engines that will
> propel you to a new place.
>
> —Ruth Haley Barton

On the evening of Monday, September 10, 2001, I sat outside on our back patio just as the sun set. John and I had been married not even three months and I talked with Mom on the phone as I did nearly every day then. I had just finished reading a disturbing book and wanted to tell her about it. We chatted about the author, about faith and family, as I leaned back against our sliding glass door, head tilted up toward the darkening evening sky.

The silhouette of an airplane flew above our condo. I mentioned to Mom how I loved to see an airplane in the sky this time of night—always wondering where they are going. Reminds me of big city living, excitement, adventure, and discovery.

The next morning I woke early to get ready for work, believing it would be a good day. The sky was a piercing blue, the color of a deep breath, the kind that looks good with orange roses—a lovely Tuesday indeed.

I drove to work listening to Bob & Sheri on the radio as I did every morning. It was such a beautiful day that I had left for work early, so I decided to sit in the parking lot with the windows down before going inside. Just as I prepared to turn off the engine, Sheri interrupted Bob mid-joke, mentioning how a small plane flew into a building in New York. Maybe the pilot had a heart attack? Poor guy.

I rolled up the window, taking the key from the ignition. The class where I was serving as a sign language interpreter didn't start for another twenty minutes, so I headed to the media center to see if there was a story about that little plane and the unfortunate pilot.

The media center was empty so I sat at the closest computer, pulled up the web browser to a news site, and waited a few minutes for the page to load. Only one story came up with a two-by-two-inch image of a tower with a hole in it, smoke coming out. There was no video and barely a hundred words of copy written beneath it. I mentioned it to the media specialist, who seemed only mildly interested. Then I closed the browser and went to class.

I thought little of it during the first class. An hour later, as I walked to the next class I noticed five instructors huddled together in a small office off the hallway, their faces ashen, electric silence hanging over them. A small radio sat in the midst of them, a somber-sounding newsperson saying words that didn't make sense, words like *attack*, *terror*, and *war*.

These were not Tuesday words.

That deep blue sky from the morning was now the backdrop for tragedy, the gray smoke of terror standing out against her brightness. Civilian air traffic was shut down in the United States for what seemed like weeks. A little internet search tells me the skies were silent for only two days, but at the time it was forever. The country was in crisis. No one felt safe. The world was ending. For so many, it already had.

Sometimes what we find on our Tuesdays is shock, crisis, and heartbreak. If we simply open our eyes it's everywhere. It's one thing to embrace Tuesday when we're in relatively pleasant places, or at least safe ones. But what about when your Tuesdays don't bring what you expect?

I think of Joseph in the Old Testament, the favorite son of Jacob, the one who had the coat of many colors. He was not in the line of Christ.

Instead, it was Jacob's brother Judah, the one who had the idea to put Joseph up for sale to the Egyptians, the one who later had three sons of his own, two whom the Lord killed because they were terrible people. And then Judah ended up getting his daughter-in-law, Tamar, pregnant with twins when he thought she was a prostitute. This was who was in the direct line of Christ, not Joseph with the coat of many colors but his lying, abusive brother Judah.

Walking by faith means being willing not to know, never to know why or how things happen the way they do, and to be willing to release my tight hold on the big finish I thought would come.

What Jesus Offers Instead of Clarity

Clarity is one of those words I've used in prayers for many years, one I've held on to like a tattered lovey, a comfort when things seem dark. I'll be all right if I could just get some clarity.

In nearly every major and sometimes not-so-major decision, I've prayed for clarity. Once when that didn't seem to work, I even Googled "how to make a decision." I'm not saying I'm proud of it, I'm just saying it's true.

But lately, every time the word comes out of my mouth in prayer, I hesitate. I'm realizing for me, clarity can be a nicer word for control. If I could just see the future, I could make a good decision about this part of my life.

Often when I say I want clarity, what I mean is I want to have a peaceful feeling about this decision. I want to know the right answer, to know I'm making the right choice. And I desperately want to take out all shades of gray when it comes to making this decision, want clear lines and long views and big pictures. I want to be able to state my desire but I don't want to be disappointed. I can become so focused on making the right choice that I forget to acknowledge what a gift it is that I can make a choice at all.

I forget to receive the gift of grace, to remember how Jesus is with me and has made my heart his home. I forget I can trust him with my life and trust myself to choose well regardless of how unclear things may seem. I forget that my true home is an invisible kingdom I can't find on a map.

I'm not saying I won't get peaceful feelings or right answers eventually, but when I make those the goal, decision making becomes a lot more frustrating. And that conversation in John 14 comes rolling over my soul, when Thomas said, "Lord, we do not know where You are going, how do we know the way?" (v. 5).

The most logical response of Jesus would have been, "I'll show you the way, I'll show you the truth, I'll show you your life." We would like that and it would seem loving and make sense and comfort everyone. It would comfort me. It seems like that would be the help and hope people need.

Instead, though, Jesus simply says to Thomas, "I am the way, and the truth, and the life" (v. 6).

He didn't say, "Come to me and I'll give you answers." He said, "Come to me and I'll give you rest." And maybe we'll still get the answers; maybe he'll show us the way even while he is the Way. But I think he is telling Thomas something important about life and he tells me this as well.

That feels hard. That seems like the long way. If the Way is a person, then I'm not sure I understand. If the Way is a person, my ability to control or manipulate outcomes or shortcuts is greatly hindered. If the Way is a person, I have to admit it isn't me.

But even in this, in the midst of the questions and disappointments, I recognize the faintest sense of longing, of wanting to know Christ not only as my way to the Father but as my way of life. With Peter, I remember, *Lord, to whom shall we go? You have the words of eternal life.* I want answers. Christ gives me himself along with everything I need for life.

Jesus prayed in John 17 as our High Priest—boldly—for the Father to be glorified. This was his deepest desire. But he also prayed in Gethsemane, "Father . . . let this cup pass from Me" (Matt. 26:39). His soul was walking through a deep disappointment. But in Gethsemane, the sweat of his desire met the blood of his disappointment. There they mixed beneath him, turning a pale shade of red, mingling so deeply with one another they could no longer be separated.

When I am willing to explore my deepest disappointments I might be surprised to find my deepest desires lingering just beyond. Knowing Christ may only be possible when we come face-to-face with our deepest desire and are willing to walk through our deepest disappointment.

In Matthew 6:11, Jesus also prayed to his Father, "Give us this day our daily bread," but I want bread to last the month. He invites me back, again and again, to ask only for grace to last through nightfall and no longer, trusting more will come tomorrow.

One question I ask myself before I pray for clarity is this— What do I want even more than clarity?

Sometimes I can't answer that because there's nothing I want more than clarity. In a way, this is an answer all by itself, telling me something important to know. Maybe I'm worshiping clarity rather than Christ. If I always had clarity, why would I need faith?

The Sacred Act of Sitting

I talk about the fog; I doubt that's even the best word to describe this season, but it's the only way I've been able to name it. I accept these seasons are part of normal life and part of growing up too. I'm learning more about what it means to have faith without depending on certain kinds of feelings to go along with it. Sometimes faith *feels* like nothing.

This soul of mine has been churning the transition my family is in, turning slowly, shaking out distraction, seeing what's left over now that the dust has settled. Some of the identities and certainties I have held on to for years have fallen gently away.

While some seasons of change are more pronounced than others, aren't we always moving from one thing to another, beginning and ending and middling? Life is made of transition and the soul is always processing something. We do well to remember to leave a little breathing room for the motion and the desire and disappointment that inevitably tag along.

And so we look for benches on the edge of the fog, not for a place to escape from the questions but a place to sit even in the midst of them. The simple act of sitting is becoming a kind of metaphor for me, a way to practice faith when things feel hectic or when truth doesn't feel true. Nothing fancy or hokey, but intentionally sitting down with the reality of the moment and refusing to talk myself out of it can bring quiet discovery of what I long for, what I fear, where my hope burns most bright.

Sitting with Marion again, I share with her about a relationship that has faded away, one I used to hold dear but now is basically non-existent. I tell her I fear it was my fault, that perhaps I did something wrong but don't remember, and if I could only figure out what that fault was, I could repair it.

I'm doing the hard work of trying to manage an outcome as well as uncover a reason for everything. And the effort is eating me. It is having me for lunch and dinner and breakfast and afternoon snack.

I say I have faith, things hoped for but not seen, but when I really burrow down deep into my soul, I wonder. Faith doesn't mean waiting for understanding or clarity. Faith means trusting God in the midst of misunderstanding and lack of clarity.

I've learned to stop trying to earn my acceptance, to release the idea of a rules-based religion. I've learned what it means to let go of the try-hard life. But daily, I still need to learn to let go of *life*. I don't live with life that comes from me, but with the life of Christ within me.

> Our hearts are hungering for the *Sacrament of Letting Go*. Once we discover that we already possess enough grace to let go, trust begins to form in the center of who we are. Then we can take off our shoes and stand empty and vulnerable, eager to receive God's next gift.[1]
>
> —Macrina Wiederkehr

I confess how disappointed I am that I don't have clarity. But in the confession, I begin to see Christ. I begin to release my obsession with building my life into something linear, something I can figure out. Instead, I believe that letting go doesn't mean I'll be left with nothing. It means I can more fully hold on to Christ and trust in the life he is building within me. I sense him inviting me to trust him, not because I'll finally understand, but because I'll begin to believe he understands me.

Marion asked me if I would consider telling myself a different story about the ending of that relationship, and after I thought in the silence, I finally answered her: "I don't know what other story to tell."

"Maybe there's no story at all. Perhaps it simply *is*."

As a woman who likes to know the reason for things, it's difficult to accept things without an explanation. It's one thing to acknowledge I'm disappointed, but to admit there may be nothing I could have done to prevent it is a deeper disappointment still.

We like to talk about celebrating the gifts we have been given, but facing the losses is important too. Not to wallow, but to keep company with them long enough to recognize what part they play in our story, to name them, and eventually release them in the presence of Christ. Before we move too quickly to hope, it's important to grieve the losses, to handle them, face them, and let disappointment do its deep work.

If we are willing to follow them, our disappointments will lead us to our deepest longings. They are the sparks we needed to start the flame of desire. And in that place of longing, we may finally discover what we truly long for more than anything else.

Living on the Corner of Desire and Disappointment

On Christmas Eve, I consider the with-ness of Christ; how he left all his glory in heaven and came down to rescue us. He came as a baby—so unlikely. Is this really the Messiah, drooling on the hay?

John and I sometimes feel this dark space in front of us, the emptiness of a map or a plan. Our question echoes that of John the Baptist, *Are you really the Expected One, or should we look for someone else?*

With Thomas, we ask, *We don't know where you are going, so how can we know the way?*

If Colossians is true, then Christ is before all things, and in him all things hold together. Including me. So I cannot separate myself out from my desire. Or my disappointment. John and I are building our home at the intersection of desire and disappointment. Maybe that is the most honest thing we can do—to embrace both sides of our experience and realize we may never be able to pick just one. It's a tightly wound tension, to be sure. My city-building ways want to turn my back on all the disappointments, but the bench dweller in me invites me to head out on the road to the invisible kingdom and find what might be just beyond the heartache.

When I am honest with myself about what I most want, I must also confront the reality that what I most want I cannot have. Or at least, I *may* not have. The reason why it's terrifying to admit our deepest longing, the reason why I seldom allow myself to do it, is because too often it seems that longing leads to disappointment in the form of a glaring life-limitation I have little control to change. Desire makes us vulnerable.

Sometimes those things we most want aren't tangible like a pretty home or a healthy family. Sometimes what I want more than anything is to be fully understood, to be able to explain myself, to have everyone see where I'm coming from and to have it all turn out well.

I tend to categorize my emotions the same way I organize my drawers, trying to put like things together, to separate the jeans from the pajamas. If I'm sad I can't also be happy, if I'm longing then I must not be satisfied. But I'm learning in this upside-down and inside-out kingdom of spirit beings walking around in broken bodies, we are not just one way.

Sorrow and peace shake hands in the corner with laughter, anger, and fear. Desire and disappointment often keep company with one another on the bench.

You can realize this in any number of ways—laughing at a funeral, pain during childbirth, crying at graduation. We have all experienced the reality of a multicolored life, of living with the *Thank God* as well as the *Please, God*. Of walking through the right now and the not yet.

You may realize this on your everyday Tuesdays in your own backyard or, like I did, in the backseat of a bus on a trip to

Africa. You can be riding in that bus with your travel companions in a foreign country, bellies full with fries and a burger, talking about television shows and silliness and movies you've seen lately.

And within seconds, you notice the road change and you hold on to the seat in front of you, and in the background somewhere, you think you hear a drumbeat but you can't be sure because that doesn't seem to fit, exactly. But you are in Uganda after all.

You steal a glance out the window and realize you've arrived at the Katwe slum in Kampala, but you put off accepting that for just a few more moments, knowing the desperation will shock your soul and despair will cling to you like children, one on each leg.

But as soon as the bus stops, you see a marching band of children through the cloud of dust and garbage, with a trombone and drums and a tuba. And they're playing a song you recognize, but "This Is the Day that the Lord Has Made" doesn't fit here. Don't they know? And where did they get a *trombone*? You don't think they realize the oxymoron they are, because they play loud, swing back and forth to the beat, and so all you can do is get off the bus and grin like a fool, march straight through despair like you don't know any better, and sing along.

Hope and grief, all mixed up together, just like that. You feel the desire of what could be right alongside the disappointment of what is. And so you gather them both up and take them by the hand because you have a parade to attend.[2]

A Prayer for the By-Faith Walkers

We confess our unwillingness to be naive, our desire to know who, what, where, why, and how. We confess our fear of desire, knowing how it, too, often leads to disappointment. But we desperately want to long for you above anything else. And we know that sometimes you show yourself in ways we don't expect. As we sit on benches at the corner of desire and disappointment, as we stand at the crossroads of our longings and our limits, may we have the kind of sight that sees things un-seeable. May we experience the longing with which you first longed for us.

CONFESSION & LAUGHTER

Why Lightheartedness Is the Truest Kind of Miracle

When one is a stranger to oneself then one is estranged from others too. If one is out of touch with oneself, then one cannot touch others.

—Anne Morrow Lindbergh, *Gift from the Sea*

One day last week I'm struggling through those old kinds of struggles that never seem to fully go away—self-acceptance, over-thinking, fear. My mind cycles through them as they sit on the lazy Susan of my soul. Pick one up, turn the wheel, put it back again.

So the Susan is spinning at the rate of the world and John walks in to my sunroom office to ask me a simple question and I snap at him for interrupting me as if he had just told me off or insulted my hair or said I looked fat. In fact, he only asked me if I needed anything from the store.

My response has nothing to do with him and everything to do with the discouragement festering in my own soul, but I immediately feel both terrible as well as strangely justified.

After we talk through it, after I apologize, after I turn back to my desk to continue my work, I am forced to face the state of my soul. My first response is shock—*I can't believe I just did that.* My second response is shame—*What a terrible person I am.*

Shock and shame are my most natural and immediate responses when I make a bad choice or have a bad reaction. My shock and shame response is a better indicator of the condition of my own soul than having the bad thought or choosing poorly in the first place. If I feel shocked and ashamed when I snap at my husband, maybe I am assuming I can handle life on my own and don't need redemption, not really. And so when my soul has a bad idea, *I can't believe it.*

Shock and shame are my response when I forget where heaven is, when I forget my true home isn't a throne but a bench, when I forget what really happened at the cross. But redemption doesn't come from worrying over what a terrible person I am or wringing my hands about the terrible thoughts I have.

It's one thing to consider the events of the crucifixion from a historical perspective, that this really did happen to an innocent Jesus all those many years ago. It is another thing to consider myself among Christ's executioners. And there I stood and still stand to be sure, considering myself as one able to judge when I have no righteousness of my own to fall back on. In my flesh, on my own, I smash the truth I see of myself in his presence. I cannot look upon my own inadequacy with peace. It is too terrible.

But it is yet another thing altogether to look at the truth of Scripture and remember this: *When he died, I died.* And so instead of watching from thousands of years later or even standing among the dirty crowd who killed him, Jesus brings me closer. He put me on the cross with him—my old self, my sin, my terrible reflection. But while there together, he hid me within him and absorbed the punishment on my behalf. And so he set me free.

My true life-perspective is one of a dead person who has been given life again. Who could be freer from the worries of this life than one who has died? While our flesh remains as we walk on the gritty earth, our spirits have been made new. I need a daily reminder that the crucifixion wasn't just something that happened to Jesus. It's something that happened to us.

> For if we have become united with Him in the likeness of His death, certainly we shall also be in the likeness of His resurrection, knowing this, that our old self was crucified with Him, in order that our body of sin might be done away with, so that we would no longer be slaves to sin; for he who has died is freed from sin. (Rom. 6:5–7)

From Shock to Confession

Shock and shame keep my head a clean distance from my heart. That is a dangerous place to live. I don't want this kind of disconnected life. The answer isn't to shame myself into better thinking. That never works.

Instead, I want to stop being shocked by my own capacity for terrible thoughts and bad behavior. Until I stop being shocked, I will continue to gasp and gawk at every foul thought that comes into my mind. I will constantly point to some imaginary version of myself and then return to my real self and the incongruence between the two will bring only dizziness, discouragement, and hopelessness. My soul simply can't survive the whiplash.

I have an insane capacity for jealousy, selfishness, hoarding, backstabbing, criticism, revenge, and procrastination. The answer to dealing with the shocking thoughts and behavior I'm capable of is to refuse to be shocked in the first place. Instead, confess and turn toward love. Be loved. Be small. Belong to Christ.

I want to learn to keep company with my weakness even as I practice walking in the New Way of Christ. The only way I know to do this is to confess, both my sin and Christ's righteousness—to continually accept my capacity for sin, but embrace my potential for health, restoration, love, forgiveness, patience, and hope in Christ.

I want to remember I am capable of making bad choices while also bearing in mind the baffling choice of God: he chose to make his home in me even though he knew exactly what he was getting himself into.

I want to always see my ability to choose the old but rejoice in my freedom not to.

I want to be aware of the darkness but identify with the light.

Refuse to be shocked, confess your smallness, and receive grace, forgiveness, renewal, and belief.

From Shame to Laughter

While mopping the floor one afternoon at her house, my mom moved a chair away from the wall and noticed the molding near the floor looked strange. She tapped it with her foot and the wood immediately gave way, crumbling onto the hardwood. The culprit? Termites, those tiny insects that feed on dead plant material.

Termites are also known as "silent destroyers" because of their ability to chew undetected through wood, flooring, and wallpaper. Termites thrive in the darkness. None of the insects or rodents we so despise seeing around our houses are as dangerous as termites. They can single-handedly destroy the foundation of a house in just a few short years. Lucky for my parents, they spotted the insect early and the damage was minimal. Still, they had to treat the house to the cool tune of nine hundred dollars.

When I'm stuck in shame, my soul becomes like the baseboard in my mom's house—unstable, battered, eaten through. I long for a lightness of heart that heals the soul, but the shame won't allow it.

I've been reading Brennan Manning's *Souvenirs of Solitude* in the mornings. His chapter called "Really Human, Really Poor" has been on repeat for several days just because I can't get over how true it is. He speaks of being poor in spirit but resisting self-hatred, something I have struggled with understanding. He tells this story:

> Distracted after a disturbing phone call, I left the monastery to give a talk to the inmates of Trenton State Prison and began with the outrageous greeting, "Well, it's nice to see so many of you here!" And so it goes. Frequently not in form, on top, or

in control. That is part of my poverty as a human being, and self-acceptance without self-concern simply expresses a reality. An impoverished spirit prevents the poor man from being a tyrant to himself.[1]

I tipped my head back and laughed out loud all by myself. There was no wringing of hands or heavy anxiety for his having misspoken. There was no shock over his ill-timed comment or shame over his own thoughtlessness. There was only an acceptance of the reality of his own frailty accompanied by his refusal to hate himself for it.

On the level of my soul, I long for this kind of lightheartedness. I take a few deep breaths in. In this delicate place of embracing my humanity without despising it, I find a kind companion in Christ.

Two Surprising Ways to Cultivate a Light Heart

Sundays have never been as calm as they are now. It's a sad commentary on our pastoral family, I know. It seems like those who work at churches might be the most spiritually formed, the most centered, the most eager to walk through the church doors. It isn't true. But you already know that.

Last week as we drove to church (as a family! I'm still not used to this!), one of the kids mentioned something about being bored on our way. Our church is only a ten-minute drive from our house, so boredom was not the core issue here.

I held my tongue and faced the window, rolling my eyes as hard as I could because I am mature and motherly. But my husband the pastor, ever more willing to meet our children right where they are, spoke a few words of wisdom as we made our way down Spring Garden Street, next to the railroad tracks.

He told them two things we need to learn how to do that are hard but will serve us well in life. Number one, we need to learn how to be bored. Number two, we need to learn how to recover from embarrassment.

Well, those are two lessons no one taught me in school. But as I thought more about what he said, I realized those two, simple, Tuesday type of lessons might help us be formed into the likeness of Christ more than any big, remarkable, mega lessons ever could.

How Boredom Can Lead to a Light Heart

When the kids were toddlers, one of the hardest things for me to do was to get on the floor and play with them. They wanted to play house and I would try to be the sleeping dog or the sick baby, but they caught on to my lazy ways fast and always wanted me to be the mommy. *Always* the mommy.

I don't know when play became such hard work but it truly is because it is boo-rrring. I would rather clean out my closet or scrub the bathroom sink than play with Polly Pockets. It takes hard work to be bored gracefully.

When John said to the kids that we need to learn how to be bored, he was talking about kid boredom, the kind that comes during weekdays when it gets dark early but they can't watch television because it's a school night and there is nothing, *absolutely nothing*, to do.

In their minds, boredom equals doing nothing and maybe that's the point. Moving into boredom, instead of trying to avoid it, is generally the very action that transitions them out of boredom. It forces creativity, imagination, and wonder.

But it's harder for me to apply this to myself. I wonder, when was the last time I did nothing? Checked off nothing? Accomplished nothing? Spoke nothing? Bought nothing? Planned for nothing? Making room for boredom insults my need to produce. And it seems like a strange and immature goal. Grown-ups don't get bored.

Since John left his position at the church, he has had to walk through some vocational boredom. Though he still has creative ideas, desires, and motivation, he doesn't have an outlet for them. And so he's forced to wait. This has proven to be a deep and abiding lesson for his otherwise producing-prone personality and one for me as well.

I started to change my mind about boredom a few years ago when I was in a conversation with a pastor of a small church and listened to him explain what his typical day looked like: "I sit in silence, do some study and sermon preparation, meet with people, and am bored." The bored part is what got me, because the highly programmed environment I'm used to doesn't allow space for boredom. There is always something more to do.

"They pay me to be me." He said he doesn't have respect because he's the pastor, but he has respect because he's himself. Part of his freedom of being himself is resisting the temptation to fill every minute with productivity and allowing a little margin to be bored.

I'm learning to practice stillness more regularly, to leave some room for sacred silence when I can. John's words reminded me of my desire to continue to learn how to be bored well, how to bring my nothing into the presence of Christ and simply be with him—no agenda, no checklists, no accomplishing allowed.

As it turns out, being bored can be super hard work. But it's the very work of boredom that reminds me that I don't, in fact, make the world go around. My agenda isn't the most important one and, many times, may not be important at all. Knowing this is a great first step toward cultivating a lightness of heart.

How Embarrassment Can Lead to a Light Heart

I have a chronic embarrassment problem. If I am at a wedding (let's just say) and it gets late at night and I've had a little too much chocolate with a side of a crowd of people, I talk way more than is necessary. I want more than anything to be in a room by myself in the quiet, but instead of retreating, I advance, much to my own great horror. And I watch myself start to babble or become irrationally chatty and then I start over-explaining my not-funny-in-the-first-place jokes because I'm just so tired.

The bottom line is when I'm uncomfortable and/or over-peopled, I get chaotic and twirly on the inside and I fluff moments in the conversation the way you might fluff pillows on a sofa and later think back on the moment and wish I would have just stopped saying all of the words. I end up saying things I regret. Not reputation-ruining things. Just little, dumb, unnecessary things. So embarrassing.

But at least I showed up at that wedding. Several years ago I was enjoying a lovely Saturday with friends, took the kids to the park, pulled some weeds in the yard, had a girls' night out with good food and a movie. And then on Sunday, we went to church, the kids were happy, we had lunch out, and then I had some quiet moments alone at home.

I sat down to clip some coupons and there, beneath a stack of that week's sales advertisements, was an invitation. To a wedding. Of a friend. For yesterday. As I held it in my hand, I could feel the blood rush out of my face, that creamy card stock mocking me with its swirly, silvery writing, silently accusing me with yesterday's date. I'm even a little anxious telling you now.

My first instinct was to think of someone else to blame, anyone but me, anything but my own lack of organization, failing to transfer the wedding date from the card to my calendar. *Surely* it was the bride's fault for failing to call all her guests and remind us to come to her wedding!

Talk about feeling shocked and ashamed. I couldn't escape it. While I was stuffing my face with chicken Florentine pizza with my girlfriends the night before, another friend was getting married and I missed it because I forgot.

The next week, I ran into the bride's mom at church and she immediately asked if everything was okay. "We missed you at the wedding! We figured your kids must have gotten sick at the last minute. I know it's so hard having young kids at home." Oh the grace she offered! I couldn't handle it. I have never wished one of my children was in the hospital except for in that moment. I thought about lying and making up a really good and forgivable reason why I wasn't there. But I couldn't do it. Instead, I confessed to her how much I regretted not being there and the truth was, I forgot the date.

It was so embarrassing but also disappointing. I wanted to be there, to celebrate, to meet my friend's husband for the first time, to be a good friend. I messed up and I couldn't take it back. I immediately went out shopping, spent way too much on a wedding gift, and wrote a card of apology. But then came the hard work of waiting for my feelings to return to normal and the color to return to my face. This takes effort, the kind that is invisible, the kind that comes from believing that my identity is not wrapped up in my mistakes or my successes, my organization or my lack-thereof. I felt small when I realized my mistake and smaller still when I confessed it. But the confession was a step toward releasing the shock and the shame.

When we begin to get present to our small moments, we become aware of how those little moments are forming us. We talk too much. We put our feet in our mouth. We forget to go to weddings. Instead of brushing these off as unimportant annoyances, I want to invite Christ to join me in these uncomfortable places, these small red-faced moments, these places that are usually passed over because I honestly want to forget them. It doesn't mean I have to change my personality and stop babbling at weddings or overreact to my mistake of missing one. But I can begin to see these moments as part of my whole life and discover how Christ wants to meet me in these small, obscure, annoying moments.

This is the hard work of letting Christ twist my shock over my own mess-ups into confession in his presence. And eventually, turning my shame into laughter. Eventually.

Rather than resenting my weakness, I believe Jesus is asking me to confess my weakness. Being poor in spirit doesn't mean despising self but releasing self from the expectation of being anything but poor. Small. Helpless. Worn.

How many times have I been embarrassed but covered it up by shrinking back or lashing out? What connections and experiences have I missed because I'm either remembering a former embarrassment or fearing a new one?

In these moments, my soul needs to remember to turn away from the city of self-preservation I'm so tempted to build and turn instead toward the kingdom of God, where I might mess up again, be embarrassed again, feel shame again. But this act of turning is the most important soul exercise in the life of a believer. It's called confession and it looks like this:

Don't try to handle your anxiety. Bring your anxiety into the presence of Christ.

Don't try to fix your loneliness. Bring your loneliness into the presence of Christ.

Don't try to hide your addiction. Bring your addiction into the presence of Christ.

Don't try to change your attitude. Bring your attitude into the presence of Christ.

Don't despise your humanity. Bring your humanity into the presence of Christ.

There is still responsibility and action that comes from me. But my action is not to make right, to make whole, or to make better. My action is to usher my abilities, inabilities, failures, and successes all into the presence of Christ.

How Boredom and Embarrassment Led Me to Laughter

In the middle of a busy speaking season, I was invited to give several talks at a large women's conference. The first of the three went as expected and I looked forward to speaking again the next day.

The second day of the conference I was scheduled to do the same talk back to back for two separate sessions. My session was all about breathing in a breathless world, about finding Jesus in the small moments, a lot of what I've written here in this book. I visited the room a few hours before the women arrived and was surprised at how big it was. At least five hundred seats were set up. *They must be expecting a big crowd*, I thought to myself. I went back to my hotel room to freshen up and review my notes.

When it came close to my session time, I headed down to the room again. As I stepped off the elevator, I heard a low rumble of laughter and conversation, assuming my room had already started to fill. But as I got closer, I realized it was the room next to mine with all the people gathering inside. Walking closer, I realized why. A sign at the opening of the workshop next to me read: Igniting Sexual Intimacy in Marriage.

Of course.

And then, it got better. Not only was my room not packed, it was nearly empty with maybe ten people scattered throughout. And though it filled to around thirty by the time I began to speak, I still felt somewhat silly standing on a big stage talking to such a small crowd.

Ordinarily this wouldn't have been a huge issue. After all, I'm the woman who is telling everyone that smallness is a good thing. I often enjoy and even prefer the intimacy of a smaller group. But clearly they expected more to show up based on the number of chairs in the room. And clearly the conference organizers did not consider the implications of putting a talk on living art and embracing smallness next to a standing-room-only workshop about the most interesting topic on the planet with only a paper-thin wall to divide us.

So as I'm talking about small moments with my soft voice and my inspiring photos, she's next door talking about sex. By the way, did you know sex is *hilarious*? Their laughter was deafening. I was sure that every woman in my session wished she had chosen sex over smallness. Just as I was tempted to dismiss us all so we could run next door and learn all about funny sex, I heard a distant rumble from somewhere in the room, soft at first but growing ever so slightly—like a rhythm, like a growl, like a *snore*.

I continued with my talk while scanning the room to find the source, and there near the side was a woman asleep. And this wasn't one of those oops-I-fell-asleep-and-woke-myself-up-with-a-polite-snort kind of sleeps. We're talking REM sleep here. *Dreaming*. Her snore grew so loud every person in the room turned to look. And even though everyone noticed, no one seemed eager to wake her up. And so I continued to talk for several minutes over the snoring and the muffled laughter from next door until finally, mercifully, someone woke her up.

I don't know the woman's story and I certainly didn't begrudge her that nap. But here's one thing I thought as I stood up there to finish my talk: *I bored her to sleep.*

While I continued to make my points and finish my talk, a mounting sense of discouragement grew in the back of my mind. *There are exactly two and a half interested people in this room and I'm tired and also sick of the sound of my own voice and all I really want to know is when will this be over?*

In the predictable way that art mirrors life, it was also during this time that I was working on this book, the one about leaning into my smallness rather than running away from it. Can I tell you how badly I wanted to run away from that room? Can I tell you how deeply I wished I was someplace else?

I think I just did. But I can also tell you that after that workshop was over (and a second one just like it because, remember, I had to do it twice. Oh the humanity!), I went to meet a friend and we laughed until we cried. And a mere hour after it happened, it became "that time I put everyone to sleep next to the wild sex talk" moment.

I was thankful for community that day. I was thankful for laughter that day. More, I was thankful for the snoring and the sex talk that reminded me, more than anything had in a long time, that my smallness is a gift, a reminder of how Christ keeps company with me—not only in every ordinary moment, but also in the ones that make my face turn red.

The Kind of Hero Our Soul Really Needs

Stories tell us a lot about our real lives. They teach us about friendship and loyalty, love, and loss. They teach us what it looks like to be brave and what can happen when we're not. The heroes in stories often start out as the underdog: the nerd, the weak, the poor, the lonely, the invisible, the forgotten, the bullied. And then something happens where he has to make a choice that will result in consequences from which there is no return and we then see the strength that exists deep within.

It's ingrained within us to root for the small guy, but no one wants to be him in real life. When I think of my childhood heroes, several come to mind, none of them small. Wonder Woman, because of her beautiful hair and awesome powers. Dorothy Gale, because of her ability to travel over rainbows and kill witches. Beverly Cleary, because she wrote stories about a girl I could relate to. And Atreyu, the brave boy warrior in *The NeverEnding Story* tasked with saving a dying empress from certain death.

One reason why these are heralded as heroes in my mind is they remain untouchable, either by virtue of their beauty, their power, their talent, or their task. They are brave and courageous in an obvious sort of way.

As important as I think it is to have heroes we look up to, it's equally important to have heroes we look over at.

> Charlie Brown must be the one who suffers, because he's a caricature of the average person. Most of us are much more acquainted with losing than winning. Winning is great, but it isn't funny.[2]
>
> —Charles Schulz

It's one thing to create a hero who is lovable, admirable, and dashing. What isn't so easy is to create a layered character (especially a cartoon one) who is chronically embarrassed, rejected, and made to look like a fool and still have him come out as the hero. But that's what Charles Schulz did with Charlie Brown. We relate to him in his embarrassment and chuckle at his consistent misfortune.

But the heroic part of Charlie Brown is that the kid never gives up.

Charlie Brown doesn't ride in on a white horse or save the world in a blue cape, but he endures in the midst of everyday difficulty and that's the kind of hope most of us need.

Like Charlie, we need to know how to carry on as the manager of the team even when our team keeps losing. We need to learn to trust our friends even though the football has been pulled away more times than we can count. We need to learn that love is still an option even though the little red-headed girl doesn't look our way. We need to continue holding out our trick-or-treat bags even when all we get is rocks.

True hope doesn't come from good results, positive outcomes, or sure wins. The hope that is deep and enduring is knowing we will be okay even if the results and outcomes *aren't* a win.

Charlie Brown is a Tuesday hero for the soul.

He makes embarrassment okay, even endearing. He gives me permission to be small and humble but also inspires me to persevere. That's the kind of hero I need when I'm discouraged on my everyday Tuesdays.

We all recognize the kinds of miracles Christ worked on earth—giving blind men sight, barren women children, deaf people hearing, a virgin a baby, and dead people life.

These are mega miracles. But when it comes down to the bench level, the kinds of miracles that make a difference on my Tuesdays are when Christ turns my shock into confession and my shame into laughter.

As I learn to sit down on the inside, on the bench in my soul with Christ, I realize the most natural result of confession and laughter is that others come along on the journey. A soul can't be light alone. I need people, as difficult as that sometimes can be for me. But as he moves within me, I'm drawn to his movement in others. Important things happen in my soul as I sit on my Tuesday bench with Christ. What kinds of things happen when I gather my bench with the benches of others?

A Prayer for the Charlie Brown Soul

Even as we accept our own frailty, help us not to despise ourselves for it. Instead, may our weakness be a reminder of your strength within us. Embolden us to speak even if we misspeak. Enliven us to move even if we fall down. Encourage us to embrace even if we get hurt. Work Tuesday miracles in our midst by turning our shock into confession and our shame into lightness of heart. As we face those places in our souls that are frozen, may the hard spots begin to thaw in the presence of Christ. May we not try to mop up the water that comes from the melting but offer it to somehow quench the thirst of someone else.

Our Tuesday Soul

Questions for Bench Dwellers

1. With whom in the Bible does your soul most closely relate today?

2. Consider some questions you're asking in your soul today. In what ways might they change if you were willing to pray them?

3. As you stand at your own intersection of desire and disappointment, what do you see?

4. Have you ever moved too quickly to hope, forgetting to let disappointment do its deepest work?

5. How do you generally respond to embarrassment: laugh it off, shrink back, or lash out?

6. What connections and experiences have you missed because you are either remembering a former embarrassment or fearing a new one?

Part 5

Seeing beyond TUESDAY

More love. Less fear.

Happy work is best done by the man who takes his long-term plans somewhat lightly and works from moment to moment "as to the Lord." It is only our daily bread that we are encouraged to ask for. The present is the only time in which any duty can be done or any grace received.

—C. S. Lewis, *The Weight of Glory*

In this section you are invited to:

- be led by love rather than pushed by fear
- embrace small beginnings
- see beyond small endings
- live well in ordinary time

UISION & CONTENTMENT

Learning to Let Love Lead

God can do anything, you know—far more than you could ever imagine or guess or request in your wildest dreams! He does it not by pushing us around but by working within us, his Spirit deeply and gently within us.

—Ephesians 3:20 Message

I have a recurring dream of being expected to be somewhere but not showing up on time. It's often math class. The bell has already rung, I take too long to remember my locker combination, and then once I finally open it, I realize I don't have my math textbook.

I roam through empty hallways mid-semester, looking for a math classroom that I quickly realize I've forgotten to attend all year. If I don't wake up in a sweat by now and actually make it to the room, I am further shamed once I realize my homework paper is blank and I don't understand one thing the teacher is saying.

A lot of decisions I make in my waking hours are to avoid feeling in real life like I do in my math dreams. I want to be prepared, ready, and in control. And so I make plans.

There is a real tension for wanting to live fully present on our Tuesdays but also knowing that our lives cycle through seasons and Tuesday isn't all there is. How can we live fully on our Tuesdays while, at the same time, plan for the days ahead?

In my own life I'm discovering most of my plan-making can be categorized in one of two ways: either I plan as I'm pushed by fear or as I'm led by love.

Pushed by Fear

Fifteen years ago, I'm working at a local high school as a sign language interpreter. It's morning and the bell rings to end the first class of the day. I gather my bag, thankful for the few minutes I have before the next class begins. I make my way to the teacher's lounge for a quick phone call. Just as I'm hanging up to rush to where I need to be, the principal's voice comes over the intercom, announcing a tornado has been spotted in the area and everyone should stay put. I instinctively turn to look out the window behind me, surprised to see my own reflection staring back instead of the front lawn of the school. Outside it is dark as night and it's not even ten in the morning.

Later we'll learn the storm, with wind gusts reaching just above 80 mph that May morning, wasn't necessarily impressive according to the F-scale, but it still comes in as the worst Greensboro has seen in twenty years. My drive home that afternoon was filled with detours as I was careful to navigate around downed trees and power lines, the aftermath of the day the sky turned black.

My apartment wasn't damaged and neither was my car. The school day eventually continued and my nephew, born later that day, is now almost fifteen. Though it was fifteen years ago, I think of that storm often because there is a tree in our neighborhood where someone carefully carved these words: The May 25 2000 Big Storm.

This tree bears the mark of memory. I don't know how the storm affected the person who carved the wood that day, but it was enough for them to take the time to mark it.

When I walk past this tree on the trail near our house, I think of that day still—how the principal had to make a choice for the sake of safety to keep the students inside, how the sky turned black and ominous, how we couldn't change the weather, only try to stay out of its way.

There is obviously an element of fear in something as unpredictable as a tornado. Fear pushes us to take cover and wait for it to pass over.

But it's possible to live like a storm is ever brewing just outside the door even when the sky is clear and bright. It's possible to take cover even when there's nothing to take cover from, to plan for extremes and complications even when the day in front of us is simple and straightforward. This is the kind of pushing that fear does and it often shows up like a heavy idea or a recurring thought in the night.

It's possible to live as though every move you make is an anxious attempt to avoid an unwanted consequence rather than a thoughtful decision to move toward life. When I'm pushed around by fear, my life becomes one marked by hiding from the potential storm of loneliness, failure, isolation, invisibility, or insignificance. Take cover or the storm might overtake you. Avoid danger. Sit under the banner of fear.

Who has time for benches of connection? I need to build a city for protection.

I've done it. Oh dear, how I have done it. When the kids were little I lived in fear a lot. I was afraid they would get sick and it would never end, afraid I would get sick and not be able to take care of them, afraid of making the wrong decisions about where we should live, how we should school, if I should take a job or not.

When my first book came out and speaking opportunities started to roll in, I said yes more than I maybe wanted to because I was afraid of missing out on something. I also said no a few times because I was afraid I couldn't pull it off. Fear pushes both ways, you see—keeps you from doing things you might want to do and convinces you that you have to do things you don't want to do.

When fear bullies my soul, I know it because I spend lots of time wishing I was someplace else.

- I become obsessed with building my life.
- I am frantic to catch up.
- I feel like I'm missing out.
- I search but don't have hope of finding.
- I build but don't have a vision for finishing.
- I strive but don't believe I have what it takes.
- I compete.
- I compare.

- I hide.
- I feel ashamed but I don't know why.
- I refuse to move toward others.
- I dread small beginnings.
- I look at other people's eight-foot assignments.

When fear pushes me around, I feel small, the kind I want to run from. But I can't because the ground beneath my fast-moving feet feels more like a treadmill than a path that leads somewhere. Just the same old working with nothing to show for it. These are the bruises that come when our souls are being pushed around by fear.

I can't prevent storms from coming, but I can decide not to invent my own. I like the idea of marking a storm like the tree-writer did. *This happened, it was bad, and we lived through it.* But I want to let go of the habit of making storms and giving fear permission to push me around.

Led by Love

I grew up as a good girl who followed rules and did the right thing. I loved Jesus and I knew he so loved the world, but for many years I didn't truly know his love for me. Though my relationship with him was real and full of true faith, it was often too structured and boxed in. I trusted him. I prayed and knew he was with me. But I saw him as a faraway outline of perfection, a distant lover of the world, of the prodigals, and of the people who had real problems.

I was a good girl who did things right. I desperately wanted him to notice me while, at the same time, I never felt like he did.

It is sometimes impossible to see the thin places in our lives in the midst of living them, in the midst of feeling looked over and ignored. But there are a few distinct times I can point to in my life timeline and say, *There. That is where God came near and showed himself right where I was and not where I thought I should be.*

Like one night in early college when the drama of being nineteen was overwhelmingly too much. I walked from the library to my dorm room, overcome with trouble and worry and angst. On my way, I passed a bench and was compelled to stop. I sat down there waiting, tilting my head back to stare at a black, starry sky. As the tears came I asked God to show me what to do next, and I perceived the words in my spirit as if he was sitting beside me: *I love you.*

That wasn't what I wanted to hear. I wanted answers, solutions, and closure. I wanted a city plan. *Can you give me that?* And as if it were written with stars on the canvas of a deep night sky, he spoke of love again and again. I didn't fully receive his love that evening. I walked away frustrated and heavy. But that bench was a thin place for me, a place I have often looked back on and pointed to as a reminder that the God who made the universe not only sees me, but loves me; not because I'm good but because he is. For the rebels as well as the rule-followers, his love is the same. And he meets us in quiet places whether or not we see him there.

Being led by love has to start by recognizing we already have it. I can't let love lead if I don't know it's there to begin with.

I recognize now how God invites me to sit on benches almost daily. They look different from the one outside my college dorm, but his message is the same.

On the bench right outside my front door, I'm thankful for the Tuesday home I have this day. I know it may not always look like this white siding with those black shutters, but right now it does. And I'm thankful for both the cul-de-sacs with the aging neighbors as well as the gates leading to new places I can't predict, control, or map out yet.

On the benches I'm building in my work every day, the kind I'm ever trying to manage and control, I'm learning the importance of keeping my eyes on my own work. I'm finding relief when I stay within my eight-foot assignment. Spotlights, attention, and success are nothing in the presence of Christ. Rather than turn from the pain of smallness, I can turn toward Christ and partner with him in every small thing.

On the benches of community, I'm learning what it means to be honest and mature with myself first and then in the presence of others. I'm learning that I won't move perfectly, but that must not keep me from moving at all. And my movement needs to be focused on building benches of connection rather than building walls of protection. If I'm competing with you I cannot connect with you. I'm learning I have a lot to learn from children.

On the bench inside my own soul, I *know* God is with me more than I *feel* that he is with me. This part is hard, especially for a feeling-oriented girl like me. But walking through fog, questions, uncertainty, and transition is good for my inner life as I'm reminded where my true home is—Christ in me, my hope.

I want to have a vision for the future that is shaped by love, not driven by fear. I admit, I'm not exactly sure how to do that. But I do know that sometimes I'll be going along on a regular Tuesday morning, doing my regular Tuesday things, and I'll have an overwhelming flash of desire for something that doesn't exist yet. I'm learning that the tension between a hopeful vision for the future and a solid contentment with the now has a lot to do with that flash.

The Discipline of Chasing the Flash

Driving through the mountains on a foggy day, you know you're going up, you can feel the rev of the car engine as it pulls and digs tires into the pavement beneath you. But you can't see the view because of the fog. With your eyes trained on the centerline, you can see enough road to continue forward. But then, unexpectedly, the fog lifts and you catch a glimpse of the view—green, rolling hills to your left, tiny houses in the distance, a range of peaks straight ahead, a river cutting her way through the rock. Instead of simply traveling the road in front of you, now you've caught a glimpse of where you're headed.

Spiritually, that's how it feels sometimes. Life goes along as normal, but then we experience a clear moment when the fog of life lifts and we have a hint of a whisper, a flash through the ordinary gray of what we want, how we wish to live. We walk into a thin place between heaven and earth, like someone cleaned the dark glass for just a moment and offered us a peek into the truest reality, heaven one inch above the ground.

Maybe we hear a lyric, engage in a conversation, read a line in a book, and for a moment we have to turn off the music, pause in the conversation, or put the book down because we have been so profoundly moved by how this artist in front of us has articulated the purpose for which we know we're here. And we wonder why we don't always see the world this way, why we can't live with kingdom eyes at all times.

But then the phone rings or we'll get up from our chair and pass a mirror in the hallway and notice the pounds we've gained. We'll move into the laundry room and see that new shirt that needs to lay flat to dry, the wall we want to re-paint, the memo with the grocery list.

These daily reminders are good and right, for these are the stuff of our Tuesdays and this is where we live. But even as I practice living within my Tuesdays, I'm learning the discipline of chasing the flash. Because that's exactly where the flash happens—on those ordinary days.

In her book *The Memoir Project*, Marion Roach Smith also describes these glimpses of understanding on a topic as *flashes*, simple connections in an otherwise disconnected world. She's talking to writers about writing, but I think this concept applies to a lot of things:

> Mere flashes are all the understanding you need bring to the writing table. Because when you have a flash of understanding on one topic, you can write an essay. Write an essay and you tackle a scene. Master the scene and you can write seventy-five of them and have yourself a book.[1]

As a writer, facing a whole book is a daunting task. As a human, facing a whole life can feel that way too. Especially when you become aware of desire, of a hope and a movement deep within you but maybe aren't sure what next steps to take in walking in that hope. You want to embrace a hopeful vision for the future without sacrificing a healthy contentment with the now.

We don't have to see the whole picture at once and we don't have to forsake our small-moment lives. We don't have to let the pace of a fast-moving world dictate how we plan our day or our life. Instead, we can bring these flashes together in the presence of Jesus just one at a time. We can chase the flash, gather the light, and take the next step that makes sense.

I have these small thoughts of vision, hope, and desire that flash through the daily-ness like a beacon, but if I don't grab on to them, write them down, pray my way through them, or talk them over with someone I love, they quickly pass and may not return for months. The voice of God is still and small, a whisper not a hurricane. Chasing the flash is a way of putting faith into action. I may not know where this is going, but I have seen a glimpse of the goodness of the Lord.

Fear moves through like a tornado unable to discern between the delicate dreams for the future or the purposeful moments of now. God speaks in the still, small whisper. He is careful not to trample on the dreams he places within us. Instead, he waters them, walks with us toward them, and continues to give us the glimpses we need to keep on going.

A Lesson in Following the Leader

My best chance for having a hopeful vision for the future while holding on to a healthy contentment now is to let love lead. If I'm going to let love lead me into the future, I need to know what love looks like.

Lately I've been taking more walks, the kind where I put on shoes and go outside and refuse to respond to the ping. It takes more work than it should, at least for me, to release an hour of productivity and replace it with something unknown.

Will I feel refreshed after? Will it really clear my head? Will I regret this wasted time later? These questions are always a good sign that narcissistic Emily is threatening a mutiny and it's time to get into the woods and be small again.

I generally go empty-handed, although sometimes I tuck my phone between my skin and the elastic waist of my yoga pants so I can monitor how long I've been walking and how far I've gone. My measuring ways are hard to overcome. And so is my lack of cool technology and arm bands and tiny, invisible iPods.

But on a recent walk, I took nothing with me and within minutes began to think on things above rather than the things on earth. Love came to mind. And as any believer thinking about love might be apt to do, I began to mumble the verses from 1 Corinthians 13, relevant in an obvious sort of way. I didn't have my Bible or my phone, so I had to rely on memory to consider what this passage said about love. I whispered the verses to the rhythm of my footsteps, *Love is patient, love is kind.*

In other words, love sits with.

As I continued, I was prepared to recite a list of all the adjectives describing what love is, but instead I heard the words as if for the first time. This entire chapter about love only provides two words for what love is—patient and kind. Everything else in those verses is about what love isn't, what love doesn't do, or what love does.

Love isn't jealous, love does not brag and is not arrogant, does not act unbecomingly; it does not seek its own, is not provoked, does not take into account a wrong suffered, does not rejoice in unrighteousness.

In other words, love isn't a jerk.

Love bears all things, believes all things, hopes all things, endures all things.

Love moves toward.

215

And finally, as I rounded the corner near the wooden walking bridge, I began to whisper the three words that describe what love never does.

Love never fails.

The words brought tears, partly because I know they're true and partly because I don't always see the evidence of their truth in the world. Sometimes I want love to be whatever I want, whatever I think sounds nice today. But love is specific, spelled out here in the middle of 1 Corinthians. And I know these descriptions of what love is, what love isn't, what love does and doesn't do are true because when I am loved for real, the love works. It doesn't fail.

I desperately need someone to sit with me, to not be a jerk, to remind me of truth, to bear and believe and hope and endure all on my behalf. And when love moves in my presence, I know it. And I begin to re-examine my own ideas of failure and success.

But love isn't just something that happens to me, Love is someone who moves within me and invites me to move toward others.

When their load becomes too heavy, Love invites me to bend down low and bear their burden.

When their faith becomes foggy, Love invites me to come alongside and believe on their behalf.

When others can't see possibility for hope, Love invites me to stand on tiptoe and cast vision for a future none of us can quite see.

We are not promised that one day we will know the answers, have explanations, or see a detailed map. Instead, we are promised that one day we will see face-to-face.

"For now we see in a mirror dimly, but then face to face; now I know in part; but then I will know fully, just as I also have been fully known" (1 Cor. 13:12).

Love is personal. Love is relational.

I get it wrong, blame others, forget to listen, and fail to see. But Christ moves me not to push but to lead; not to force, but to invite; not to tell but to listen.

Bear, believe, hope, endure. May it be so in us. May it be so in me.

A Prayer for the Flash-Chasers

We confess our habit of creating storms. Teach us to mark them instead. May we take Love by the hand and follow gently along. May we partner with you as we look to the future; bearing, believing, hoping, and enduring. May we chase the flashes of hope that visit us in ordinary time, gather all the light in your presence, and trust you to string it together for our good and for your glory.

14

ENDINGS & BEGINNINGS

Casting a Hopeful Vision for the Future

There are no experts in the company of Jesus. We are all beginners.

—Eugene Peterson, *The Jesus Way*

When John and I were hoping for a baby, I imagined we would have a girl first. I picked out a name long before I was pregnant—Ava Grace. Once we found out we were having twins, I knew I would use that name if one of them was a girl. As it turned out, they were both girls so we had the great fun of picking out another girl name—Anna Estelle.

During all those ultrasounds before the girls were born, the babies were simply called Baby A and Baby B by the technicians. But we had names picked out, so we wanted to go ahead and assign each girl her name. Baby A was on the bottom and would therefore be born first, so we chose her to be Ava Grace since it was the first name we picked, and Baby B we nicknamed Stella.

Ever since she learned to spell her name, Ava has liked that it is spelled the same way backward or forward, like Hannah or race car. I thought of this when I read something Eugene Peterson said about God: "The way we come to God is the same way that God comes to us. God comes to us in Jesus; we come to God in Jesus."[1]

He came down to us and one day we'll return to him. In a similar reciprocal way, the gospel does this same kind of dance in Scripture, over and over again.

The first are last, the last are first.

The rich are poor, the poor are rich.

The weak are strong, the strong are weak.

This is the way of the one-inch-above-the-ground kingdom.

Jesus, the holy palindrome.

What begins small and secret may end in glory. But this glory has its own shape in the right-now kingdom, and will reap a harvest of fruit in the one to come.

Embracing Small Beginnings

There is a verse hidden in the Old Testament, nestled within a vision given to the prophet Zechariah. The chapter with this verse is confusing. In fact the whole book is. It's filled with prophecy and symbolic language and lots of history I don't fully understand. What I have learned, though, is that though a lot of the language here is deeply symbolic, it can also be practically applied to our lives today and has a lot to teach about the invisible kingdom of God.

The Babylonian armies had defeated Jerusalem and destroyed Solomon's temple. We meet Zechariah around 520 BC, over sixty years after this defeat. God's people are scattered and the few who remain are without leadership or a faithful vision. Persia eventually defeated Babylon for control of the land, making it possible for the exiles to return to their homeland once again.

Upon their return, some started the task of rebuilding the temple, knowing it symbolized the presence of God among his people and had as well been a national symbol of pride for Jerusalem and Israel during the days of its former splendor. But the economy of the time was not good, and the efforts of the few who began to build were minimal at best. They lacked vision, motivation, and resources. Even though the people were now back in their homeland, they were discouraged and demoralized.

Zechariah and Haggai were both prophets during this time in history who were primarily concerned with rebuilding the temple. Zechariah was a visionary while his contemporary Haggai was more of a pragmatist. As it turns out, the people of Jerusalem needed both of these perspectives.

The purpose of the prophets was always to draw the people who had forgotten their faith back to the heart of God. Haggai and Zechariah, though different in their approach, were united in their priorities to rebuild the temple. During this dark time in Israel's history, there may have been many who assumed God's covenant with them was no longer relevant considering their condition, the state of the city, and the destruction of the temple. They may have already given up hope, assuming God had given up on them.

The words with which Zechariah begins his sermon would have been especially powerful to the people. "Return to me, says the LORD of hosts, and I will return to you" (Zech. 1:3 ESV). His first priority was for the people to know that rebuilding the temple was important, but it was merely an outward expression of an inward reality.

One commentary explains, "The community in Jerusalem was sick at heart, and there were those who thought that a restored temple would cure all society's ills. And, indeed, the restoration of the temple would have an important role to play. But the work on the temple would become a monument to folly, unless it was accompanied by spiritual reconstruction."[2]

The prophet Haggai had the energy as well as the political know-how to get the project underway. I'm thankful for the Haggais in my life, those people who can start up projects with plans and practical applications.

But we can't forget the need for Zechariah too. He was some-one who understood that without a heart transformation, the reconstruction was in vain, a mere facade in the midst of an otherwise broken community. From this perspective, Zechariah shares a series of visions with the people, the fifth of which deals directly with the rebuilding of the temple.

In his vision, he sees a golden lamp stand with two olive trees on either side. When he asked the angel what it meant, the angel didn't directly answer him, instead giving him a message to share with Zerubbabel, who was the governor of Jerusalem at that time. The message was an assurance that the rebuilding of the temple would happen "not by might, nor by power, but by my Spirit, says the LORD of hosts. Who are you, O great mountain? Before Zerubbabel you shall become a plain. And he shall bring forward the top stone amid shouts of 'Grace, grace to it!'" (4:6–7 ESV).

These words are deeply encouraging to me. The mountain of trouble, discouragement, and roadblocks would become a plain, making a way for the Lord to establish what he said he would do. To know that the work will be completed by the Spirit of God and not by my effort means I can sit down on the inside even as my hands are fast at work. It means I don't have to keep pace with a fast-moving world even as I am engaged in the activity of it. While the circumstances in Jerusalem were specific to that time, God's principles remain changeless, and in some ways on the inside, I can relate to the despair and broken-heartedness the people experienced. Not in a physical way, but a spiritual one. Still, I can trust that the work the Lord begins will be completed by the power that dwells within me by his Spirit, not by the power that comes from me and my own efforts.

As with any project we are engaged in during our current time, this temple rebuilding project had its opponents. Not everyone thought this should be happening. They didn't share the vision of the prophets, of their governor, or their high priest, Joshua. Perhaps they believed they should rebuild the temple eventually, but not until the economy was in a more stable place.

With the critics in mind, one interpretation of God's message through Zechariah is this: "For whoever has despised the day of small things shall rejoice, and shall see the plumb line in the hand of Zerubbabel" (Zech. 4:10 ESV). Zechariah, a prophet and a visionary, anticipates a time when those who are against the project, who despise these small beginnings, will change their minds and rejoice once the temple is complete. He doesn't condemn them in anger but casts a hopeful vision for them in faith.

Another interpretation is worded a little differently, "For who dares make light of small beginnings?" (NET). This implies that anyone who hopes to accomplish something great (like rebuilding the temple to its former glory) knows that small beginnings are a necessary and important part. Who would make light of them?

And another still is, "Do not despise these small beginnings, for the LORD rejoices to see the work begin, to see the plumb line in Zerubbabel's hand" (NLT).

Regardless of which Bible translation you might read, a similar conclusion can be made from all of them—the littleness of starts is something to be celebrated and embraced, not despised and rejected.

All of this happened in reality—the building of the temple for the second time—but it was also a foreshadowing of the future coming of Christ, who himself would come to rebuild the kingdom of God and make his home in the temple of the human heart. Any work done in comparison to the work of Christ is small, even if in our eyes it looks grand and impressive.

Sometimes I wonder if I value the small starts for their own sake or if I'm holding on to the unsaid but assumed "big ending" that this small beginning silently seems to point to. I am quick to recognize the importance of embracing smallness, but do I really appreciate smallness because Christ's is the hidden way or do I value it because my soul has been seduced with the promise of big things to come in the future, imagining this small beginning will ultimately lead to greatness in the end?

It's true, the temple was being rebuilt. But the Lord is the one who would accomplish it in his way and in his timing. And it may not look the way they thought it ought to look. We have the benefit of knowing their future from this particular time in history; we know the very temple they were rebuilding in 518 BC would be destroyed a second time, just as Christ predicted when he was on the earth.

How can this small beginning be hopeful if it will only eventually lead to ruin?

I sense Christ asking me to embrace the days of small beginnings *even when they might lead only to small endings*. Because the mustard seed tells us the ending belongs to God and it is kingdom-sized. We don't get to hijack the ending with our own manufactured ideas of success. Perhaps he was speaking to his people through the prophet Zechariah about a reality bigger than the temple, about the kingdom of God one inch above the ground, about the invisible reality that was truer than any visible reality they could hold on to.

Seeing beyond Small Endings

Once Zechariah is finished sharing his visions, the book continues with a series of sermons, the second of which is presented in chapter eight. There he shares a prophetic message for things to come in the future.

Zechariah tells the people that the Lord promises to bless Jerusalem, saying, "I will return to Zion and dwell in Jerusalem. Then Jerusalem will be called the Faithful City, and the mountain of the Lord Almighty will be called the Holy Mountain" (8:3 NIV). This sounds like a grand event, sounds like something that would require bright lights, stages, headlines, and attention. This kind of hope sounds like a big deal. This ruined, defeated city will be called faithful? What will that look like?

In my own imagination, it seems he would then detail the reign of a powerful, gallant leader who will come back and build a kingdom for the people.

But he doesn't.

Will God send an army to rebuild their lives?

Nope.

A talented speaker to fill arenas?

Nope.

An organization to launch an impressive program?

Nope.

Bear in mind the Tuesday truth of this community of Jerusalem at this time: they were broken and still recovering from war. They had returned to their land, but most of their older generation had either died in exile or on the return trip home. Those who had already passed on would have been the people who remembered the former glory of Jerusalem before the Babylonian defeat. The current community is one that had likely watched their parents and grandparents die. Without them, they lacked the perspective of the past or the wisdom of their current situation.

Likewise, many families who had young children may not have made the dangerous journey from exile back to Jerusalem, not wanting to put their families at risk in a land that was broken and destroyed.[3]

This is the reality of the lives of the people during this time. Zechariah knows this well and so does their heavenly Father. God's vision for Jerusalem was not that a powerful leader will come and build a kingdom or that an impressive army will dazzle and remake old things new.

Instead, Zechariah paints a simply beautiful picture of hope for the people, one they would have been hard-pressed to imagine considering the ruins of their current situation:

This is what the LORD Almighty says: "Once again men and women of ripe old age will sit in the streets of Jerusalem, each of them with cane in hand because of their age. The city streets will be filled with boys and girls playing there." (Zech. 8:4–5)

The Message translation is especially meaningful for me:

Old men and old women will come back to Jerusalem, sit on benches on the streets and spin tales, move around safely with their canes—a good city to grow old in. And boys and girls will fill the public parks, laughing and playing—a good city to grow up in. (Zech. 8:4–5 Message)

We have a God who is specific in his vision and intimate with his offering of hope. His people needed to know that their generation would continue and that the joy of children would once again fill the streets of their beloved city. They needed to glimpse the benches of the future in order to grab on to hope for the broken benches they sat on now.

This isn't a city the people will rebuild by their own might and power like Enoch, the city Cain built when he turned from the presence of God. It's not a city they will manufacture with their own blueprints and agendas, their own committee members and politicians.

God doesn't purpose to destroy their city but to *rebuild* it, in his timing and in his way. As their hearts return to God, their city will be called *Faithful*. At first glance, the vision for their future sounds like a small ending—old people and children?

But the encouragement the Lord gives his people is specific to them—that their oldest and their youngest would dwell in joy and wisdom together, would sit on benches and play in streets. Sitting and playing, a picture of the kingdom of God.

This would not have sounded like a small ending to the people. To the remnant of Israel that had recently returned from exile, those who had lost their elderly parents to death and perhaps left their young families behind, this would have sounded like a miracle—the simply Tuesday kind.

The Beauty of Sitting as We End and Begin

I mentioned before how the simple act of sitting is becoming a kind of metaphor for me, a way to practice faith when things feel hectic, foggy, or when truth doesn't feel true.

When considering the endings and beginnings you're walking through, it helps to sit and consider what you no longer have to hold or what you'll soon need to let go.

You're not technically a pastor's wife anymore. How does that feel?

They don't seem to understand. How might you be misunderstanding them too?

He's graduating. Where does that leave you?

She's growing up. What are you afraid of?

The job doesn't feel like the right fit anymore. Do you need to move on?

He left and you don't think he's coming back. Is it time to let go?

Have a seat and consider the disappointments as well as the celebrations, the fears as well as the joys. Let's open our eyes to the benches that line the moments of our lives, broken as they may be. Let's allow God to cast a hopeful vision for our own cities, not the kind we're building with our own hands but the kind he's building within us—the kingdom kind.

Here are a few places I've been sitting lately.

I sat on a bench with a book and a journal at a local park, but I did more staring than reading. I watched the moms and babies stroll by, the workers with their good intentions toward the public bathrooms, the guy on his bike who rode without a helmet. I read a little about David, how he was both a man after God's heart and a killer. I thought about how none of us are just one thing, but many shades of light and dark and shadows of gray, proof that we need Jesus.

Sitting alone does good work.

I sat in the front seat of a rented Ford Focus that I paid one million dollars to borrow for the day and panicked when I first got in because the seat was too low and I couldn't figure out how to adjust it. *How do they expect me to drive if I can't see over the dashboard!?* But then relief when I found the right button and the seat raised up and all was well.

Sometimes you sit in unfamiliar places and it takes some adjusting to get your bearings. You drive alone on unknown highways and cry as you listen to cartoonist Roz Chast talk about her aging parents on the radio.

Sitting in unfamiliar seats listening to other people's stories does good work.

I sat in an uncomfortable airport seat, waiting to board the winged, sideways skyscraper, remembering that I can't hold it up with mind games or willpower. So instead, while waiting to board the bus in the air and shoot out into the wild blue sky, I ate an apple and read an article about Sandra Oh leaving *Grey's Anatomy.*

Sitting on the edge of my comfort zone does good work, especially when the seat is thirty thousand feet above the ground.

I sat for several meals across from a friend, one of my favorite writers, Shannan Martin, a gift from the internet. We traipsed and meandered through town and conversation, sitting on cement benches and vinyl restaurant chairs, sprawled on the end of white-duvet-covered beds.

Sitting with a friend to hear and to be heard does good work, especially one who shares your fears and, more importantly, your dreams.

I sat in a fancy office chair, stared out a window at the city beyond, and had to accept that even though I needed to get work done, I didn't want to be a relentless dictator over my soul if my productivity didn't meet my expectations. Even while I'm doing the work of counting words and crafting sentences, Jesus just wants to be with me and this is the kind of work that means something even though I can't measure it.

Sitting with my weakness, my obsessions, and my profound ability to twist art into achievement—this does good work too.

I squeezed myself onto a swing in my neighborhood during a morning walk, thought of the ways our life used to look compared to how it looks now. While some of the changes are encouraging, others are not so easy to categorize. I recognize my desire to evaluate everything even as I appreciate the mystery of being unable to. I thought of the future and the past and where my hope comes from.

The rhythm of sitting on swings does good work, a reminder that we are tethered even as we sway.

I sat with Stella at the kitchen table, quiet while she spelled her words, frustrated over my frustration, ready for the school year to end. I answered the questions I could, aware of how soon the day will come when her homework is beyond my ability to advise. She's moving on and I can't always go with her. But while she's here, I'll sit beside her.

Sitting with family does good work even when we can't help them solve their problems.

When we sit we may find answers, but most likely we'll finally hear the questions. We may uncover things we'd rather avoid, things like fear, anger, weakness, or entitlement. But we might also find courage, peace, and hope there too.

When we sit, we let what is be, we remember to release outcomes or at least finally admit how tightly we are clinging to them. When we sit, we let ourselves be human.

When we sit, we may realize that an ending doesn't have to mean the end. Maybe it simply means it's time to begin again.

A Prayer for the Small Beginners

We confess how we often despise the days of small things. We confess our surface desire to hijack endings with our own ideas of success. Our patience only lasts as long as the results we can measure. But you spin a different tale, one that gives us hope in a future we can't see but know is coming. In you, we have everything we need to walk through small beginnings wherever they lead. Teach us to sit on benches as we take the long way home.

TUESDAY &
EVERYTHING AFTER

Living Well in Ordinary Time

> Benches are cool. Sacred by design. Benches are often a
> place where something special happens and important
> talks take place.
>
> —Amy Poehler, *Yes Please*

I stare out the morning window, the outline of my tired head staring back at me, wispy hair out of place, wild. The sun isn't up yet; only the faintest, faded line of pink lingers over the trees out back. *This slow rising happens every morning*, I think to myself. As I wrap my hands around my warm cup, my mind rushes into the day ahead. Even though the house is quiet, I'm running on the inside as if things are in full swing. My feet haven't moved but my soul is rumbling.

But this intentional practice of embracing smallness on the inside is beginning to shape my life. When I start to feel the edges of my soul shake with anxiety, when my hands reach for my pen to make another list, when my eyes long for the city lights to light the path in front of me, I am slower to trust those first instincts. I've become oddly suspicious of ambition, especially the kind I find in me.

Tuesday has become my teacher, and her lessons are basic, simple, and free. I will take my cues from Christ as he reveals himself to me in my Tuesday moments, and this is what I hear.

Discovering Our Tuesday Home

Like you, I'm figuring out how to walk with Christ into my day, into Target, into church, into the kitchen, and most importantly, into the lives of other people. Christ doesn't stop being relevant just because I'm standing at my sink, cleaning out my closet, meeting over coffee, driving to the bank.

I'm learning that in those moments when I most desperately want to be shown what to do, where to go, and how to choose, Jesus's most specific answer to me is not a what, a where, or a how, but a who. He offers me himself and my first, most honest answer is *Thanks, but no thanks. I'd prefer a map and a schedule.*

But the God of small things is my gracious companion even if he is a lousy travel agent.

I read these words from Brennan Manning: "I don't expect and I don't like a God who comes to me in failure, in loneliness, in poverty. Yet God comes to me where I live and loves me where I am. If I am not where I am, God cannot meet me. It's as simple as that. But when I remain where I am with everything that is moving inside me, salvation comes."[1]

So then the question becomes this: *Where am I and what is moving inside me?* I know I don't need to ask God to join me because he's already with me. But inviting him anyway feels hospitable. It feels like something a friend would do. Sometimes that's what prayer is—simply inviting God to join us where we actually are, not because he isn't already here but because inviting him reminds us that it's true.

Dad once told me that every time he walks his dog in the morning, he sets the calendar in his mind. Today is *Tuesday, January 27*, he'll whisper to himself, imagining the week, where the day lands within it, where it stands in relation to the month, the season, and the year. I laughed when I first heard that. Dads can be so weird. But then I realized I do the same kinds of things, intentional practices that help me get present—not to where I wish I was or where I think I should be but to where I actually am.

When I get caught up in planning for later, it helps to sit on a bench and remember where I am. My version of "setting the calendar" is this. I pull out my journal and at the top I write five words: *These are the days of . . .*

And the rest of the sheet I fill with a list including everything that comes to mind that represents our current season of life. Today, for example, my list looks like this:

These are the days of
Praying about middle school.
Writing my fourth book.
Celebrating new beginnings.

Eating mint chocolate chip ice cream with John once the
kids go to bed.

Sunday night community group.

Planning for John's new ministry.

Watching pink sunrises.

Being the tooth fairy.

It's simple, I know. But a few moments to reflect what these
days actually hold—rather than what we wish they held—is a
practical way to celebrate our smallness and welcome Jesus into
our actual life. The items on your list are clues to the kingdom.
Christ is in us, and that means our moments are the earth address where he chooses to live.

As you purpose to sit on the bench right outside your door,
what do you see? These are the days of . . . what?

Embracing Our Tuesday Work

As the sun continues to rise, I remind myself that relief will
neither be found in continuing to chase an ideal of my productive self nor in shaming myself for my inability to get everything done.

I think of yesterday and smile. It was a good day—a nice
blend of productive as well as reflective. I was kind to myself,
which is unfortunately not something I can always say. But the
kindness influenced a lightheartedness in my work that I long
for today. I look back, retrace my steps, attempt to figure out
what I did so I can package it and recreate it again today.

Instead of focusing my work efforts on building a bench for
others to sit on, my tendency is to want to build a system for

my work, to create some kind of predictable formula to ensure more good days to come.

But Tuesday teaches me that part of living well in ordinary time is letting *this day* be good. Letting *this day* be a gift. Letting *this day* be filled with plenty. And if it all goes wrong and my work turns to dust? This is my kind reminder that outcomes are beyond the scope of my job description.

John and I feel the pain of releasing outcomes as a couple as he continues to discern his next vocational steps. By now it's been nearly two years since he left his job. The first half of that time we dedicated to his rest, recovery, and establishing some new, slower rhythms for my work and our home.

But we've been watching and listening, paying attention to the benches in our own community, both the ones we're already sitting on as well as the ones we're being asked to build. John's desire has always been to serve our local community, to enter intentionally into relationships, to offer small group discipleship, and to connect with others on a soul level.

Over the course of this past year as I've been writing this book, the next step for him has slowly been made clear. He has started a nonprofit ministry here in Greensboro to connect weary souls with the gospel of grace.[2]

While many questions and details remain, one thing we know for sure is that the second half of his life and ministry will look different in form and structure than did the first half. But his desire and hope remain the same.

It helps to remember we can plant seeds but we can't make them grow. Let me hear Jesus whisper to me the lesson he taught his disciples, the one about praying for this day our daily bread, not bread to last the week. Let me believe him when he tells me the most important work I'll do today is to receive the love he wants to give and then hand it out to others.

Finding Our Tuesday People

I notice the benches outside my front window and on a whim I decide to take a Tuesday pilgrimage out to meet them. After all, here is where my neighbors first taught me about the connections that can happen if only a community has a common bench to sit on.

Curious, I grab a tape measure on my way out the door *just to see*. The sun is all the way up now, casting short shadows across the front yard, the street, and the cul-de-sac benches. As soon as I reach them, I pull the tape measure from my pocket, kneel down in front of one bench, and measure from the ground to the seat.

Fourteen inches stacked on top of each other make a high enough space to build a bench to sit on. If heaven is one inch above the ground, then the seat of a bench is the kingdom of heaven stacked on top of itself just to make a space for us all to be together.

I sit down and look up, notice the bare branches above me, the ones from our cul-de-sac tree. I remember when my brother-in-law, Frank, first talked about planting a tree. After several months of sitting on benches together during that hot North Carolina summer, we longed for the relief of a shade tree, a place that would allow us to linger a little longer.

And so one day, he worked hard to dig a hole, not even to his knees if he stood straight in it. Then he dragged that small tree into the center of the cul-de-sac and dropped it strong into that hole in the ground. We all watered, watched, wished for it to grow.

We spread blankets around her skinny trunk in the heat of that first summer, wishing she were big enough to offer leafy arms for shade and relief. She watched hot days roll by as kids played around her—lemonade stands, Barbies in the grass, not-quite cartwheels turning her upside down.

My father-in-law was still living that summer, and even though he didn't easily say the deeper things out loud, he seemed pleased that his son chose to plant a tree. He'd mosey slow through the yard, across the street, and with fingers touching around her small trunk, he'd say, "Take a picture with it every year at the same time. You won't believe how fast it grows."

In spring, she has blush white buds, four years later. And those flowers turn to leaves that will hold on until October, leaves that promise picnics, shade, and life. We look at that young tree and know it will long outlive us. But not before it bears witness to our lives and our living.

The tree, like the benches, has become a simple yet essential part of our community. It watches as the brothers stand near and remember, as the cousins play singsong handclap games, as the fathers play ball with their sons. It will watch one day in the future when the sisters-in-law cross lawns to trade sorrows and stories of their daughters driving off with their friends. It will watch long into the night as the neighbors lay sleeping and the dogs bark at nothing and the families live our family lives one day at a time. That tree will grow silently and watch our lives spin by in ordinary time. And the seasons will move around her, shape her, change her. And we'll watch her like a mirror, reflecting the growth within us.

She will surrender her leaves again, but she will still stand tall. And after that, the blushing buds that burst forth green will come whether or not we're here to see it.

She is a gift because she reminds us of our lives past and our lives to come and the life we live together as Tuesday people, sitting on benches fourteen inches above the ground.

Accepting Our Tuesday Soul

I used to think that a mature faith would bring with it clear pictures, thought that as I walked with God I would see life big, wide, and spacious. But that is not what is happening, and if you expect that, it can feel like perhaps your faith is shrinking. Because instead of being lifted up on a cloud to see the big picture, I am shrinking down into a small place, a place where I can barely see two feet in front of me, much less into next week.

Everything in me wants to fight the unveiling of the anxieties that threaten to overwhelm, push them back from showing up in my day. I want to ignore the smoky unknown; it is counterintuitive to let the anxieties rise up to the surface.

But Tuesday teaches me to let them rise up so I can release them into God's hands. Speak the fear out loud, so he can give words of truth. Don't run away from those places where it seems faith is small. Run into them, look around, and be honest about how it feels while standing there.

I leave the cul-de-sac benches to come back inside and breathe in deep the air of a new day. Truth can be a slow rising like the sun, making no difference at first. But each moment weaves itself into the next, as we believe him in the great right now, as his truth becomes a constant strand woven into the fabric of our minutes.

Today, small-moment living is sweet. Today, small-moment living reminds me of who is in control and who is not. This smallness is to be celebrated, not despised. I dare not trust myself with the next step. A mature faith says *I am desperately in need of a source outside of myself.* I always have been, but today I believe it.

Seeing beyond Tuesday

These days I am careful not to color the word *small* in negative shades, as if it were something to run from or escape. I want to start small because I'm human and dependent, not in hopes that my small will grow into something bigger. Jesus will give me the grace to stay there even when it hurts and even when it's hard. I want to stay small in his presence, not because I'm scared, but because I'm his. I want this to be a relief rather than a frustration.

Small things don't always turn into big things. But all things begin small, especially in the kingdom of God. Acorns become oak trees. Embryos become President. Life starts with a breath. Love starts with hello.

Tuesday reminds me to accept the beauty of smallness, hiddenness, and the secret work of Christ in the deepest part of who I am. I want to let him come out of me in any way he wants, no matter how it may seem to me—whether that be in one big way or in a million little ways.

While I stay small in the presence of Christ, I'm aware of his invitation to me, to stand on tiptoe and see, as my dad often says, *beyond what is to what could be.* And this doesn't mean I am to dream big and amazing things *for God.* Rather, it means I am to *believe in a big and amazing God,* period. I can trust him to be himself even as I dare to be myself.

And maybe as I do that, I'll realize that starting small isn't a means to a bigger end, rather I start small because it's what

I am. And this is good and right and holy. Who would despise the days of small things?

As citizens of an invisible kingdom, we refuse to take our living cues from the world that says to build, grow, measure, and rush to keep up. Instead we take our cues from the new hope alive within us, from the life of Christ who has made our hearts his home. We'll stop trying to keep up with the fast-moving world and, instead, we'll settle down and keep company with the small moments of our lives.

We'll pay attention to them, listen to what they have to teach us, not rush by them as if they are unimportant. We know better than that by now. We know the way these small moments link arms with one another to form the timelines of our lives. Moments: the keys to the kingdom. We know how we approach, consider, react, and exist within these small moments are indicators of how we approach, react, and exist in our whole lives. We can't afford to miss them.

We don't know where these moments might lead, what we might grow into, whom we might influence, what impact we might have. That is not our business. Instead our job is to stay right here with our friend Jesus. To know he is with us and within us, and he'll stay no matter what.

We'll find our places to call home.

We'll embrace our right-now work.

We'll gather with our Tuesday people.

We'll write our hidden prayers in the fog.

We'll let love lead.

We'll refuse to despise the days of small things and our benches will remind us why.

And even as we stand with our feet firmly planted on our Tuesdays, we'll let our souls, with childlike wonder, stand high on tiptoe with great hope, knowing the King of our kingdom will one day come again.

A Prayer for the Tiptoe Standers

May we not despise the small space we take up on earth because it is this very small place where you delight to make your home. May we not be surprised when we discover the fixed point from which you long to move into the world is not from some nebulous place out there, but rather it is from an intimate place within us. May fear, discouragement, doubt, comparison, envy, and failure not have the final say in our homes, our work, our relationships, our souls, or our plans for the future. Instead, may we live into our truest calling as people who give and receive grace, forgiveness, and love in the small moments of our lives.

Continue this day to remind us who you are. Move us forward in your name. May we turn toward hope on purpose in the midst of our regular Tuesdays and then again tomorrow.

Beyond Tuesday

Questions for Bench Dwellers

1. How do you know when you're being pushed by fear?

2. How do you know when you're being led by love?

3. What are some ways you practice "chasing the flash" or capturing those moments of hopeful vision for the future?

4. Are you holding on to something you'll soon need to let go?

5. Where are some places you're sitting today?

6. Are you hoping for a particular ending to your small beginnings?

Dear Reader,

Thank you for coming along on this journey of discovering what it looks like to celebrate our smallness in our homes, our work, our relationships, our souls, and our plans for the future.

I hope these words have been gentle arrows for your soul, pointing the way to Jesus. I hope, after reading this book, you'll never dread Tuesday or despise the days of small beginnings again. I hope you'll embrace both the gates as well as the cul-de-sacs in your own life. I hope you'll hum a tune next time you find yourself in a stairwell. I hope you'll give yourself permission to take the long way home.

On Tuesday—or any other day—if you need some company on the bench, visit me at emilypfreeman.com where I'll be writing to help create a little space for your soul to breathe. If you need some encouragement to celebrate the small, join us every Tuesday using #itssimplytuesday on Twitter, Facebook, and Instagram where we remind each other weekly how our simple Tuesdays are sacred portals to the invisible kingdom, one inch above the ground.

Thanks for sitting on the bench with me,
emily
#itssimplytuesday

ACKNOWLEDGMENTS

My deepest gratitude goes out to all the Tuesday people who have saved me a seat on the bench: John, from the moment you proposed on that bench in the Bicentennial Garden, my favorite place to sit is anywhere with you. Thank you for being the kind of man who sees the importance of Tuesday bravery, the washing-the-dishes and playing-cars-on-the-floor kind. Here's to many more years of celebrating our smallness together.

To Ava, Stella, and Luke, thank you for your excitement, your silliness, and for loving the moon in the night sky along with me. Thank you for letting me share our stories.

To Mom for taking us out to see Halley's comet and Dad for making us write that report. After moving around so much when I was young, you taught me that home is wherever we are together and for that I am profoundly grateful.

To Sherry, Susan, and James for your constant friendship, love, and support.

To all of our cul-de-sac neighbors, especially my brother-in-law and sister-in-law, Frank and Mercedes—for planting trees, for watching children, for sharing chocolate, and for being willing to let us move in next door.

Myquillyn, you're my favorite phone call, laughing partner, and big sister. You make every Tuesday better. And Chad, thank you for all the ways you have cheered me on over the years.

Kendra, you're my safest place to feel insecure. Thank you for making me cookies, for giving me courage, and for being my person.

Traci, I don't think I could have finished this book without your faithful prayers, your kind encouragement, and your administrative super powers. You and Chris are gifts straight from God's hands.

Marion, thank you for holding open a safe, prayerful space for my soul to emerge.

Amy and Lara, thank you for saying yes and for sharing the journey.

To our friends at Hope Chapel, you have been a refuge for our family during a time when we really needed one. Thank you for your faithfulness, your artistry, and your love.

And to our community group—Francie, David, Claire, Norah, Jill, Chris, Scott, Jacob, Abbey, Marianne, Walker, Angie, Greg, Kai, and Blayze—thank you for welcoming us to the table every Sunday night.

To my fellow writers at (in)courage, I feel like we've grown up together. Thank you for sitting on benches, sharing your stories, and for all the ways you've cheered me on over the past six years.

To my editor Andrea Doering and the entire team at Revell, my deepest gratitude to you for partnering with me once again to bring these words to life.

To Esther Fedorkevich, Whitney Gossett, and the entire team at The Fedd Agency, I extend a warm thank you for all the ways you champion my work. What a gift you all are.

Thank you, Sarah Masen Dark, for being an artist who makes the invisible kingdom feel real and for being the first to point out the miracle of Tuesday.

To the Starbucks at Quaker Village and the Kathleen Clay Edwards Library for offering free Wi-Fi so I could get out of my house and finish this book.

To the Chatting at the Sky readers, especially those of you who know what it means to unwrap Tuesday together, thank you for being the kindest community on the internet.

Thank you, Jesus, for arriving here small, for teaching about mustard seeds, and for saving my life.

And to you, thank you for reading these words. I hope they are kind companions for you on your journey and that they have served as an arrow for you, pointing your soul to the invisible kingdom one inch above the ground.

NOTES

Chapter 1 Cities & Benches

1. Mark Binelli, "Where Did All the Stars Go? How Light Pollution Is Stealing the Night" *Men's Journal* 22 no. 11(December 2013): 128.

2. Thank you to our friend and mentor, Steve Lynam, for this life-changing phrase, "Celebrate your smallness."

3. Eugene Peterson, *The Contemplative Pastor* (Grand Rapids: Eerdmans, 1989), 25.

4. Heather King, *Shirt of Flame* (Brewster, MA: Paraclete Press, 2011), 73.

5. Jacques Ellul, *The Meaning of the City* (Grand Rapids: Eerdmans, n.d.; reprint, Vancouver, BC, Canada: Regent College Bookstore, n.d.), 2.

6. Ibid., 5.

7. See Mark 4:26 NIV (like a man who scatters seed upon the ground); see Luke 13:18–19 NIV (like a mustard seed); see Matt. 13:47 NIV (like a net); see Matt. 13:33 NIV (like yeast); see Matt. 13:44 NIV (like a treasure hidden in a field).

Chapter 2 Moments & Time

1. Lorne Michaels, *Here's the Thing with Alec Baldwin Podcast*, WNYC radio, January 30, 2012.

2. This is a practice I still host online, but instead of doing it on the blog, we've simplified it to sharing one picture or thought on Instagram and Twitter every Tuesday using the hashtag #itssimplytuesday. Join us!

3. Kimberlee Conway Ireton, *The Circle of Seasons* (Downers Grove, IL: IVP Books), 11.

4. Ibid.

5. Sarah Arthur, *At the Still Point: A Literary Guide to Prayer in Ordinary Time* (Brewster, MA: Paraclete Press, 2011), 13.

6. Wendy M. Wright, *The Time Between: Cycles and Rhythms in Ordinary Time* (Nashville: Upper Room Books, 1999), 9.

7. Marion Roach Smith, *The Memoir Project* (New York: Grand Central Publishing, 2011), 36.

8. Eugene Peterson, *The Jesus Way* (Grand Rapids: Eerdmans, 2007), 3.

9. Ibid., 206.

10. Richard Foster, *Prayer* (New York: HarperCollins, 1992), 171.

11. "Rapeseed Facts and Information," *Soyatech*, EU Oil and Proteinmeal Industry, http://www.soyatech.com/rapeseed_facts.htm. Accessed March 25, 2015.

Chapter 3 Gates & Cul-de-Sacs

1. Myquillyn Smith, *The Nesting Place* (Grand Rapids: Zondervan, 2014).

2. There has been much discussion about whether to use *culs-de-sac* or, the more comfortable but hotly debated *cul-de-sacs*. After extensive research on the topic (including several re-watchings of *Gilmore Girls*—Season 4, Episode 10—as well as conversations with my editor and my Instagram friends), it was discovered that *cul-de-sacs* is also an acceptable plural form of the word and is recognized in the dictionary. I side with Lorelai on this one.

3. "Greensboro: History," City-Data.com, http://www.city-data.com/us-cities /The-South/Greensboro-History.html. Accessed March 25, 2015.

Chapter 4 Effort & Outcomes

1. Kenneth Coppens, "How to Germinate Mustard Seeds," *Ehow*, http://www.ehow.com/how_7012411_sow-mustard-seeds.html. Accessed October 21, 2014.

2. Claire Kowalchik and William H. Hylton, eds., *Rodale's Illustrated Encyclopedia of Herbs* (Emmaus: Rodale Press, 1998), 395.

3. Dallas Willard, *Living in Christ's Presence* (Downers Grove: InterVarsity, 2014), 15.

4. Cameron Manavian, "Top 10 Misquoted Movie Lines," *Electro Kami*, http ://electrokami.com/film/top-ten-misquoted-movies-lines/. Accessed May 4, 2011.

5. Kowalchik and Hylton, *Rodale's Illustrated Encyclopedia of Herbs*, 393.

Chapter 5 Success & Envy

1. Henri Nouwen, *In the Name of Jesus* (New York: The Crossroad Publishing Company, 1989), 10–11.

2. See Emily P. Freeman, *A Million Little Ways: Uncover the Art You Were Made to Live* (Grand Rapids: Revell, 2013).

3. Fil Anderson, *Running on Empty* (Colorado Springs: WaterBrook, 2005), xi.

4. Ibid., xii.

Chapter 6 Stairwells & Stages

1. Beth Moore (@BethMooreLPM) "1/2 I've learned along the way that to the height a person idolizes you, he/she can despise you. A switch flips & adoration turns to hatred. Never feed someone's out-of-kilter adoration. Mutual respect, affirmation & gratitude are beautiful. Godly. Adoration can turn deadly. I have

never once had a person turn out to be dangerous or disturbing and vicious who wasn't an over-the-top 'fan' first." September 24, 2014, 5:09 a.m. Tweet.

2. John Ortberg, *Soul Keeping* (Grand Rapids: Zondervan, 2014), 85.

3. Ray Romano, "The Cast of *Everybody Loves Raymond* Says Goodbye," *The Oprah Winfrey Show*. NBC, February 9, 2005.

Chapter 7 Community & Competition

1. The School of Spiritual Direction from New Way Ministries and Dr. Larry Crabb. I attended this weeklong intensive during October 2012.

2. Thomas Merton, *The Seven Storey Mountain* (San Diego: Harcourt, 1948), 194.

3. Todd Henry, *The Accidental Creative* (New York: Penguin Group, 2011), 100–3.

4. Annie Downs, *Let's All Be Brave* (Grand Rapids: Zondervan, 2014), 76.

Chapter 8 Children & Grown-Ups

1. Wess Stafford, *Too Small to Ignore* (Colorado Springs: WaterBrook Press, 2007), 211.

2. "Beverly Cleary," FamousAuthors.org. Retrieved January 22, 2015, from http://www.famousauthors.org/beverly-cleary.

Chapter 9 Honesty & Maturity

1. Adapted from Ted Loder, *Guerrillas of Grace* (Minneapolis: Augsburg Books, 1981), 52.

2. King, *Shirt of Flame*, 31.

3. Lauren Winner, *Mudhouse Sabbath* (Brewster, MA: Paraclete Press, 2003), 53.

4. Willard, *Living in Christ's Presence*, 42.

Chapter 10 Prayer & Questions

1. Parker J. Palmer, *Let Your Life Speak* (San Francisco: Jossey-Bass, 2000), 7–8.

2. John MacArthur, "Matthew 11:1–11," *MacArthur Commentary Matthew* (1989), http://www.inglesidelife.org/wp-content/uploads/2010/06/MacAurther-Commentary-Matt-11-1-6.pdf. Accessed January 22, 2015.

3. Barbara Brown Taylor, *Learning to Walk in the Dark* (New York: HarperOne, 2014), 48.

Chapter 11 Desire & Disappointment

1. Macrina Wiederkehr, *Seasons of Your Heart: Revised and Expanded* (New York: HarperCollins, 1991), 7.

2. Emily Freeman, "10 Things I Learned in January: Uganda Edition" *Chatting at the Sky*, January 29, 2014, http://www.chattingatthesky.com/2014/01/29/10-things-learned-january-uganda-edition/.

Chapter 12 Confession & Laughter

1. Brennan Manning, *Souvenirs of Solitude* (Colorado Springs: NavPress, 2009), 92.
2. Charles Schulz, "Charlie Brown," *Peanuts by Schulz*, http://www.peanuts.com/characters/charlie-brown/. Accessed March 24, 2015.

Chapter 13 Vision & Contentment

1. Smith, *Memoir Project,* 34.

Chapter 14 Endings & Beginnings

1. Eugene Peterson, *The Jesus Way* (Grand Rapids: Eerdmans, 2007), 37.
2. Peter C. Craigie, *Twelve Prophets*, vol. 2 (Philadelphia: The Westminster Press, 1985), 162.
3. Ibid., 193–94.

Chapter 15 Tuesday & Everything After

1. Manning, *Souvenirs of Solitude*, 119–20.
2. After years of praying, dreaming, and listening together, John is now the director of a local nonprofit called Grace Discipleship, a ministry that exists to connect weary souls with the gospel of grace. Visit gracegreensboro.org to learn more.

Emily P. Freeman is a writer, a speaker, and a listener who creates space for souls to breathe. Author of *A Million Little Ways: Uncover the Art You Were Made to Live* and *Grace for the Good Girl: Letting Go of the Try-Hard Life*, she also created the blog *Chatting at the Sky*, co-created the membership site *Hope*ologie* with her family, and is a regular contributor at DaySpring's (in)courage. Emily has also traveled as an advocate for Compassion International. She attended Columbia International University to study the Bible and the University of North Carolina at Greensboro, where she earned a degree in Educational Interpreting for the Deaf. She and her husband, John, live in Greensboro, North Carolina, with their three children, twins Ava and Stella, and their son, Luke.

connect with

emily

· · ·

emilypfreeman.com

ChattingAtTheSky.com

Visit **SimplyTuesday.com**
for videos, printables, and
other free resources.

"**Emily Freeman** is one of those rare writers: profoundly biblical, lyrical, transparent—memorable. Her emancipating words on these pages offer the needed keys to all the good girls longing to take wing— and soar home to God's heart."

—**Ann Voskamp**, *New York Times* bestselling author of *One Thousand Gifts*

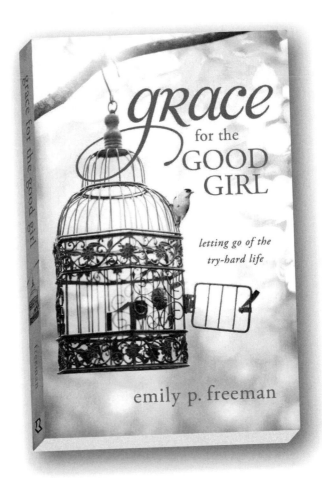

Share Emily's wisdom and encouragement with the young women in your life.

If you've been struggling with expectations—from your parents, your teachers, your friends, and even yourself—*Graceful* is for you. Are you trying hard to catch up but aren't sure what it is you're chasing?

READ AND BE SET FREE.

"Emily Freeman's luminous words hand you your rightful birthright. **Read them and exhale.** These pages just might wow you awake to **who you are meant to be.**"

—**Ann Voskamp,**
New York Times bestselling author of *One Thousand Gifts*

Do you desperately fear you have nothing to offer the world but secretly hope you're wrong?

Creating a life of meaning is not about finding that one great thing you were made to do, it's about knowing the one great God you were made to glorify—in a million little ways.

 **Revell**
a division of Baker Publishing Group
www.RevellBooks.com

Available wherever books and ebooks are sold.